Taj Mahal Through Ages

Tai Mahal - 1862

Taj Mahal-1868

Taj Mahal -1962

Taj Mahal - 2014

Anurag Mathur

1

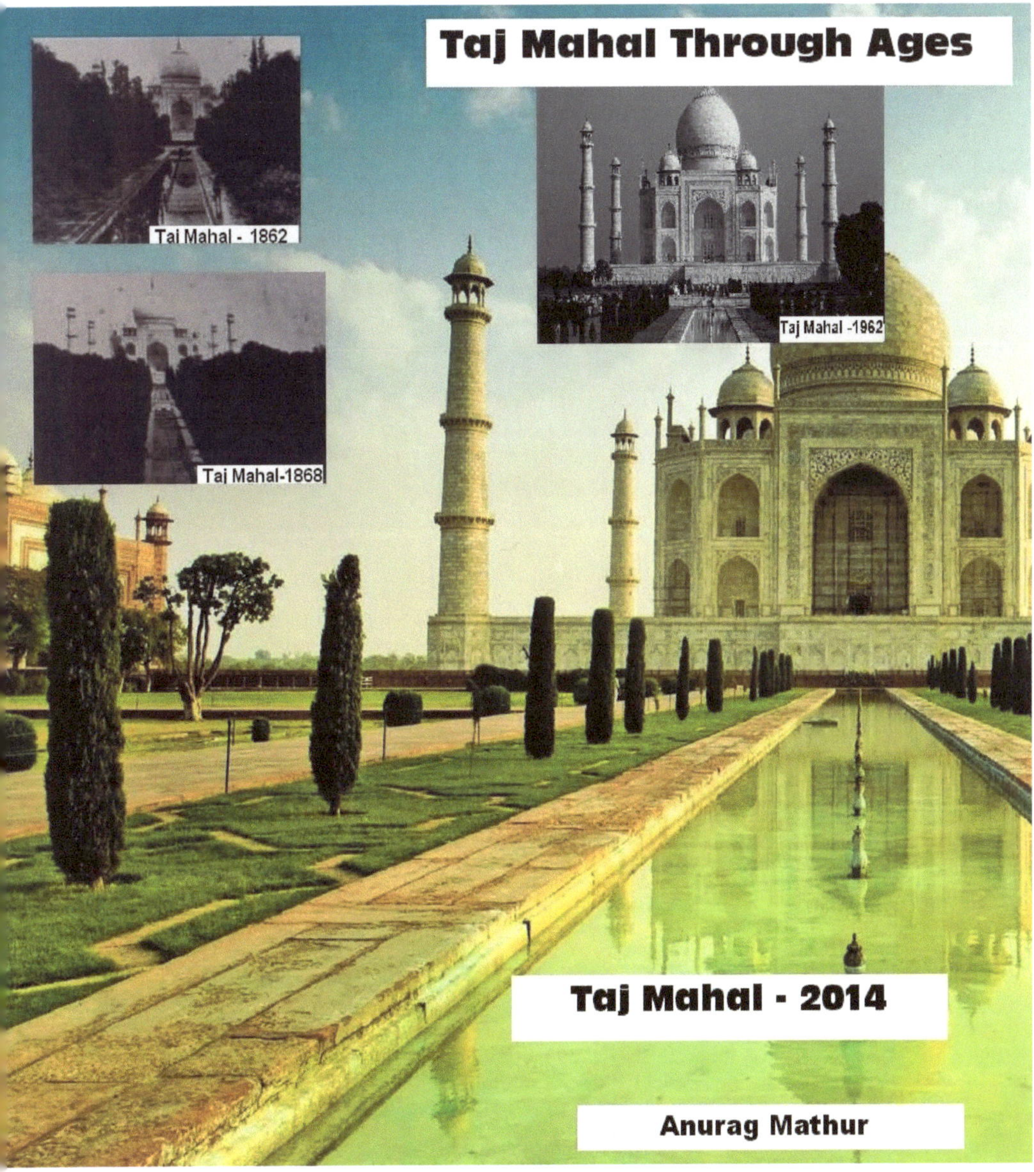

Indian Heritage Series Books --

Taj Mahal through Ages –
(Rare Amazing Pictorial journey of 150 years old, real, Black & White photographs of Taj Mahal)
WORLD HERITAGE PROPERTY

Anurag Mathur

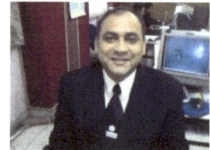

Publisher:-

About Author: - Anurag Mathur (B.Sc., M.A. - History, PhD Level Research, Post Graduate Diploma in Hotel & Tourism Management Advance Course in Tourism from IITTM – Indian Institute of Tourism & Travel Management- Ministry of Tourism Govt. of India, New Delhi & WTO (World Tourism Organization). PGDBIM (MBA-Delhi). Ex. Lecturer of History, Hotel & Tourism Management Department at Agra University. Agra & also Numismatist (Coins Collector), Philatelist, Antiques, Rare Photographs & Paintings Collector etc, Lucknow. U.P. India.

(Father of Author Anurag Mathur, Late. Shri. O.N. Mathur, Archeological Survey of India (ASI), Govt. of India -Posted at Taj Mahal & other Historical Monuments at Agra-1975 - 89. Author Anurag Mathur's forefather was posted at Royal Imperial Court of Emperor Shaha jahan as Finance Minister (Treasury Incharge –*Shahi Khazana*) as per Author's Family Tree Records & generations Chronology & rest all ancestors were educated from Kayastha family and served in Royal Mughal Court after one by one. - Indian Culture & Heritage Information, Lucknow.

Copyright Information: -

ISBN-13: 9781540552402
ISBN -10: 1540552403

Acknowledgement

By the blessings of Almighty God & Radhasoami Dayal. I am able to complete my book by extensive research and always be thankful to my Guardians Proff. Shri. Agam Prasad Mathur (M.A. Ph.D - History) Head of History Deptt. Agra College & Radhasomai Faith and Ex. Vice Chancellor Agra University, Agra. Hon'ble Shri. Subrata Roy Sahara "Saharasri" of Head & Chairman of Sahara Group & Hon'ble Shri. O.P. Srivastava, Hon'ble Shri. Alkh Kumar Singh, Hon'ble, Shri. Romi Datta, Shri. Navin Singh & Shri. Anil Kumar Pandey of "Sahara India Pariwar", my father Late Sri Omendra Nath Mathur (Retd. From ASI- Archeological Survey of India, Govt. of India), Mother Late. Smt. Uma Mathur, Friends & Colleagues. I am also thankful for Valuable support from wife Late Smt. Neera Mathur & my wife Smt. Anju Mathur and my loving Children Jitesh Mathur & Shreshtha Mathur.

Taj Mahal through Ages –

(Rare Amazing Pictorial journey of 150 years old, real,
Black & White photographs of Taj Mahal)
WORLD HERITAGE PROPERTY

Contents:-

Total No of Pages	-	79 pages
Total No. of Black & White and Color Photographs	-	50 (Appox.)

About Book:-

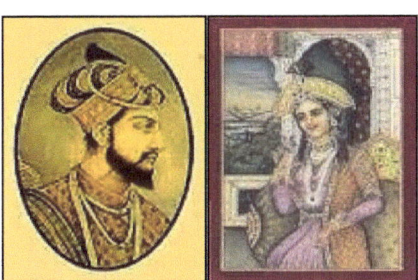

Here by this Book we would like to show you the **Amazing Rare & Real Heritage Photographs of Taj Mahal Agra** to Put an Idea about Taj Mahal, how **Taj Mahal** was looks before 150 years back? for general Awareness to Protect our valuable & Priceless Heritage of India by not destroying, Spitting, putting Garbage and not writing anything on Monuments, However Heritage Conservation is conducted by ASI (Archeological Survey of India - A Central Government Body - founded in 1861 & effectively starts working from 1870) who is responsible for Conservation, Restoration, Preservation & Reconstruction, but this is our Prime duty & help to protect our priceless Heritage for our New coming Generations for several years.

Topic 1:- Taj Mahal Fact File:-

S. No.	Description	Detail/ Name etc.
1.	Location	Agra, Uttar Pradesh, India
2.	Built by	Shah-Jahan
3.	Built in	1631 to 1648 A.D.
4.	Building Material	Makrana Marble
5.	Chief architect of Taj Mahal	Ustad Isa Afandi (Iran)
6.	Built in Memory of	Arjumaan Bano Begum entitled Mumtaz-Mahal
7.	Time taken to complete the Taj	17 years
8.	No of workers employed for the Project	20000
9.	Plan of main tomb	Square
10.	Total height of the Tomb	187'.
11.	Total height of the Taj Mahal	243'-6''(up to the finial){187'+32'-51/2''+19+4}
12.	Total cost of Taj Mahal	Rs. 4,18,48,426-7-6 {Rupees four crores eighteen laks, forty eight thousand four hundred twenty six annas seven & pies six only when gold was sold@rupees 15/-per tola(11.66 grams)} 12 pie= 1 anna 16 annas=1 rupee.
13.	Total area of Taj complex	579.2m x304.8 m
14.	Total area of central garden	304.8 mx304.8m
15.	Area of chameli farsh	970'-7"x364'-10"
16.	Height of chameli farsh	4'
17.	Height of the platform on which Taj stands	5.79m (19ft.)
18.	Area of the platform on which Taj stands	57mx57m
19.	Area of Chhakka	328'-3"
20.	Height of the Hall	80'(from the pavement to the soffit of the interior dome)
21.	Total height of the bulbous dome	145'8 ¼ (44.41m) (from the base of the drum to the apex of the finial)
22.	Load factor of the dome	748 tonns/sq.ft.

23.	Total height of the neck	39 ft.
24.	Height of the finial	32'-5 ½"
25.	Load factor of the wall of the cenotaph hall	7.9 tonnes per square ft.
26.	Load factor of the dome at its springing	12,000 tonnes
27.	Total weight of the dome	12,192.56 tonnes
28.	Total height of the minaret	132'.
29.	Dimension of Southern Gateway	151 ft.x 117 ft.x 100ft
30.	Designer of Taj Mahal	Ustad Ahamad Lahauri
31.	Superintendent of masons	Muhammad Hanif of Agra
32.	Dome Maker	Ismail Khan Afridi (Turkey)
33.	Sculptor & Mosaicist	Chiranjilal (Delhi)
34.	Sculptor	Baldeodas (Multan)
35.	Calligrapher of Taj Mahal	Amanat Khan Shirazi (Shiraz)
36.	Inlayer (Pachchikars)	Jamanadas(Delhi)
37.	Finance Minister (Incharge of Treasury)	Rai Jaggannath of Akbarabad(Agra) (Forfather of Anurag Mathur, Sahara Care Hose)
38.	Accountant general	Lala Rudradas
39.	Precious & Semiprecious stones used for inlay work in the Taj Mahal	Agate,coral, Diamond, Lapis Lazuli, Neelam, Pearl, Pukhraj, Ruby etc.
40.	Other stones used in the Taj Mahal for main gate, Main gate way, side right 'Mehman Khana'(Guest House), Left Jami Masjid (Mosque)	Red sand stone, black stone etc.
41.	Source of Water	From Yamuna river
42.	Water system in fountains & for gardens	Persian wheel system from Yamuna river just behind to the Taj Mahal. ('Rahat': Giant Wheel system pulled by Animals, which lift water from lower lavel of Yamuna river to upper level of Taj Mahal)
43.	Carving work	Floral design in marble & red sand stone on main tomb, main gate & other associated buildings of Taj Mahal
44.	Gardens design of Taj Mahal	300x300 mt. design by Ran Mal from Kashmir. Based on beautiful & Symitrical design known as 'Char bagh' pattern of those days which resembles in all most all building of Mighty Mughal Empire

45.	Foundation of Taj Mahal	Taj Mahal foundation is based on strong walled Deep dry wells of Lakhauri bricks, lime mortar & Rubble inside & stone masonry outside which supports entire weight of Taj Mahal along with safty from earth quake jurks & subsoil water level of Yamuna river which flows just behind to the Taj Mahal. Base of plastering Cement was prepared by Naturally available Tree Gums, lentils along with several hours baked small bricks called Lahauri bricks or *kakaiya Eeet*

(Source: R. Nath, Ph.D., D.D.Litt. Lecturer of History Agra College Agra & Fellow of the Indian Council of Historical Research-The Immortal Taj Mahal, 1972, Taraporaevala, Bombay)

Topic 2:- Chronology of events associated with The Taj Mahal (17th Century):-

S.No.	Date	Details of Event/Events.
1.	5 April 1607 A.D.	Betrothal of Shah Jahan to Mumtaj Mahal.
2.	10 May 1612	Marriage of Shaha Jahan to Mumtaj Mahal.
3.	17 june 1631	Death of Mumtaj Mahal at Burhanpur, temporary burial in Zainabad garden.
4.	11 december, 1631	Body of Mumtaj Mahal taken from Burhanpur to Agra.
5.	8 January 1632	Body of Mumtaj Mahal reburied at Agra.
6.	22 June 1632	First Urs in court of new grave.
7.	20 September 1632	Farman to Raja Jai Singh to expidite marble supply.
8.	3 February 1633	Farman to Raja Jai Singh to send 230 carts of Marble.
9.	4 March 1633	Establishment of 'Taj Ganj' near Tomb.
10.	26 may 1633	Second 'Urs' on foundation of new tomb, gold railing Installed around grave.
11.	28 December 1633	Farman to Raja jai Singh, awarding exchange properties.
12.	1624 to 1635	Mention of architect Ustad Ahmad, "Wonder of the Age" (Nadir al-Asr) in preface to treatise by Ata Allah.
13.	1635 to 1636	Amanat Khan inscription inside Tomb.
14.	1636 to 1637	Dated inscription on Tomb exterior, west door.
15.	1 July 1637	Farman to Raja jai Singh, not to delay marble supply.
16.	19 December 1637	Award to Amanat khan for calligraphy inside Tomb.
17.	1642	Gold railed installed around grave was replaced by exquisite Marble screen.
18.	6 February 1643	Completion of tomb complex, supervision of Makranat Khan & 'Abd-al-Karim', twelfth Urs.
19.	31 Januray 1647	Death of satti-al-Nisha khanam.
20.	1647	North arch dated inscription on Tomb gateway.
21.	Early 1649	Burial of Satti-al-Nisa Khanam at tomb complex.
22.	1649	Death of Architect Ustad Ahmad.
23.	9 December 1652	Auragzeb letter about repairs needed at tomb.
24.	31 January 1666	Death & burial of Emperor Shah Jahan at Taj Mahal.

(Source: R. Nath, Ph.D., D.D.Litt. Lecturer of History Agra College Agra & Fellow of the Indian Council of Historical Research-
The Immortal Taj Mahal, 1972, Taraporaevala, Bombay)

Topic 3:- Taj Mahal Photographs Rare and real, black and white more than 150 years Old:-

I. Taj Mahal – <u>1850:-</u> Earliest known Photograph of Taj Mahal taken by taken by Dr. John Murray of East India Company in the 1850's -Back side view taken across Yamuna River. A Man sitting at River bank:-

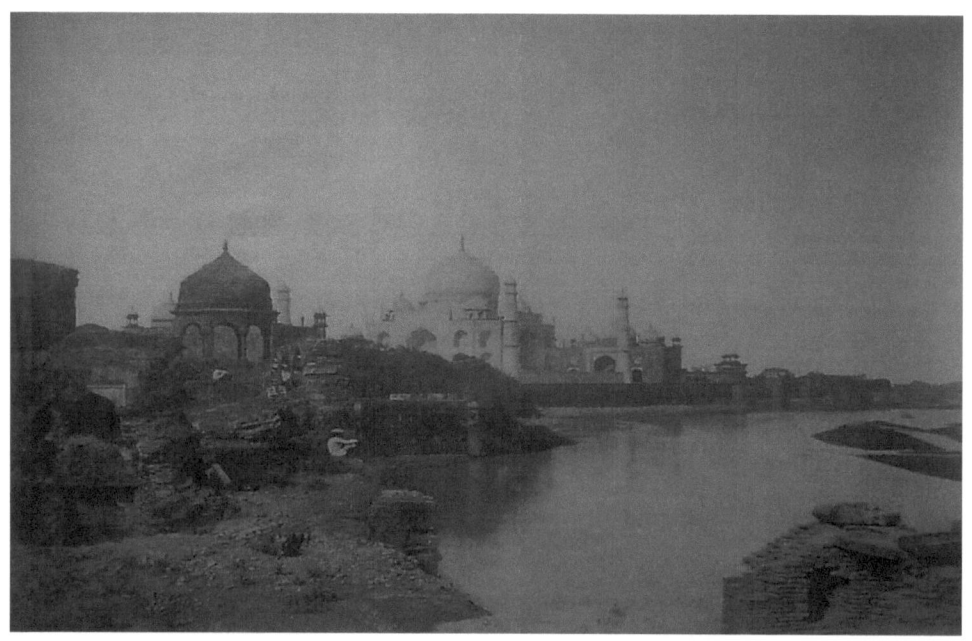

Rare & Earliest known Photograph of Taj Mahal taken by taken by Dr. John Murray of East India Company in the 1850's.

II. Taj Mahal - <u>1862</u> - with Huge Trees all around:-

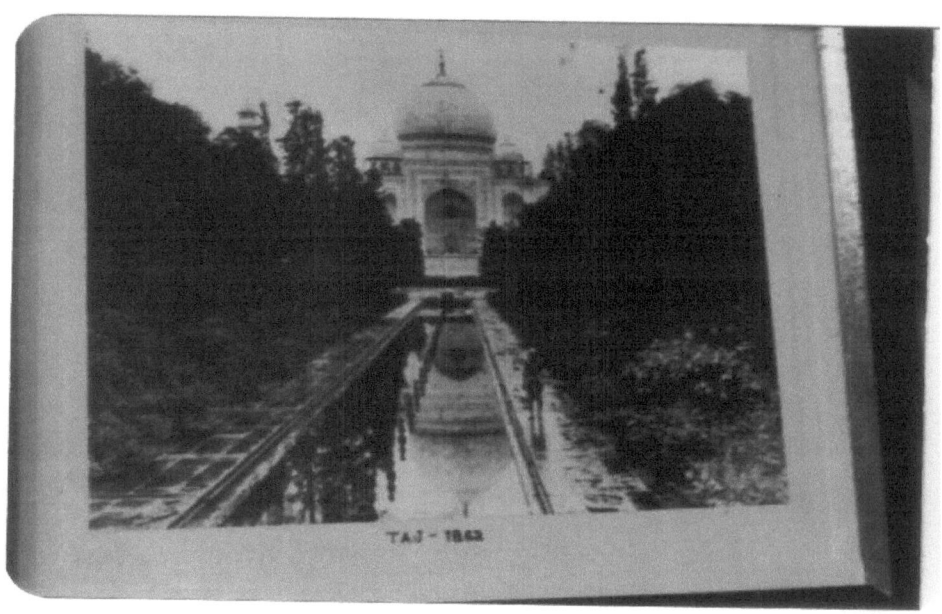

TAJ - 1862

This Amazing Rare & Real Photograph shows that what was the condition of 150 years back, there were Big trees all around & forest due to no maintenance, after some time ASI (Archeological Survey of India) a Maintenance body foundation was laid in British period in 1870.

III. . Taj Mahal- <u>1862</u>-Frontal View:-

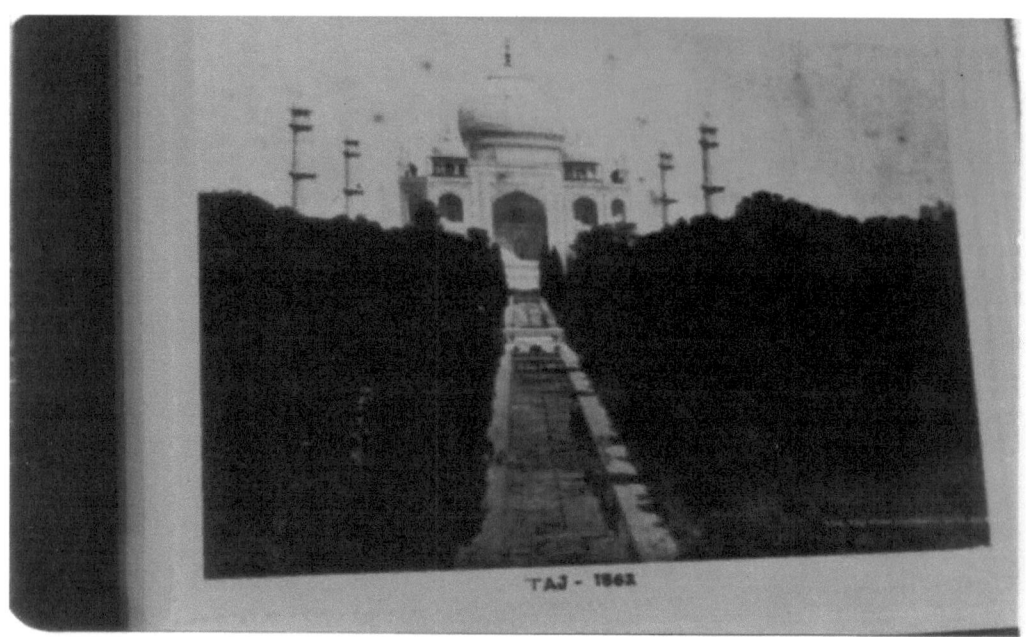

Chief Architect of Taj Mahal- Ustad Isa Afandi (Iran) & Designer of Taj Mahal Ustad Ahamad Lahauri.
Finance Minister (Incharge of Treasury)- Rai Jagganeth of Akbarabad (Agra).
(Forefather of Author Anurag Mathur), **Accountant General - Lala Rudradas.**

V.   Taj Mahal- <u>1868</u>-Frontal View:-

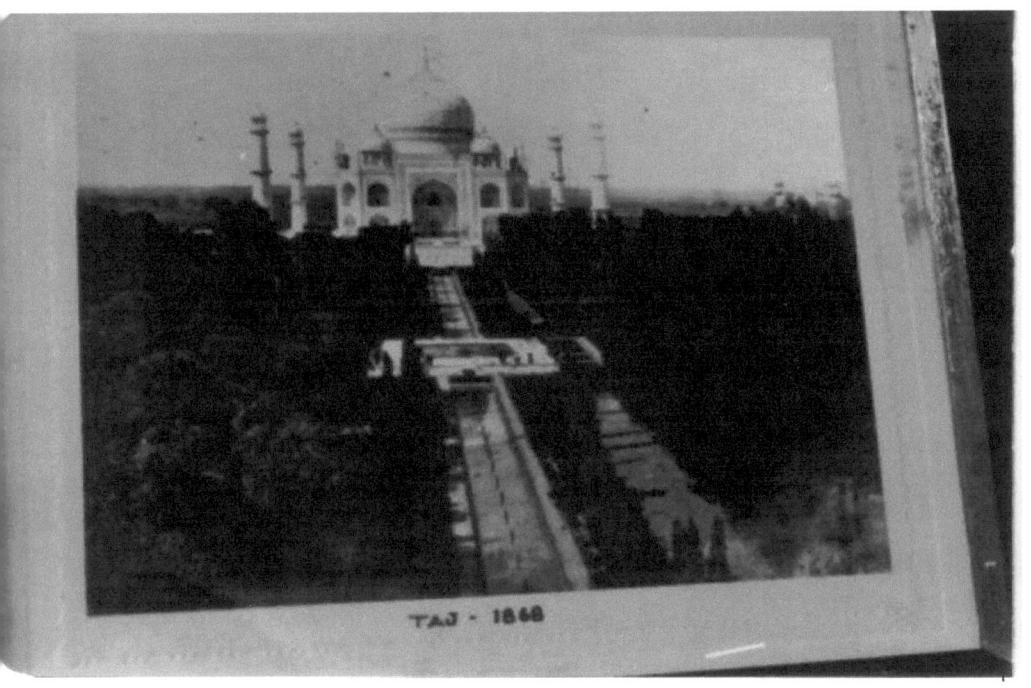

TAJ - 1868

Total cost of Taj Mahal:-Rs. 4,18,48,426-7-6
    {Rupees four Crores eighteen lacks, forty eight thousand four
hundred twenty six Annas seven & pies six only when Gold was
sold@rupees 15/-per Tola(11.66 grams)}
- 12 pie   = 1 anna
- 16 annas   = 1 rupee.

V. Taj Mahal- <u>1872</u>-Frontal View:-

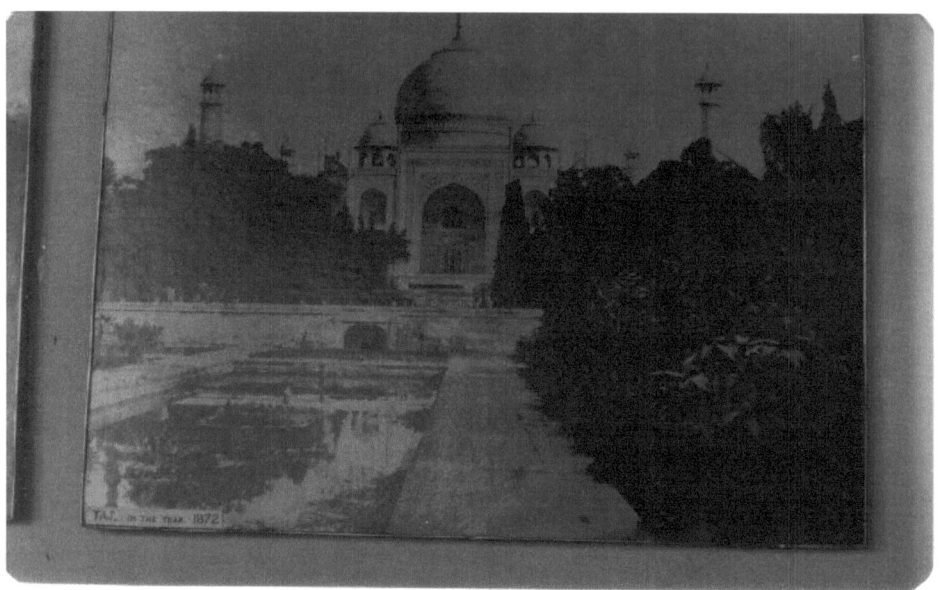

Total 28 Precious & Semiprecious stones Agate, Coral & Cornelion from Arabia, Diamond from Panna, Jasper from Punjab, jade & Crystals from China, Lapis Lazuli & Sapphire from Srilanka, Neelam, Pearl, Pukhraj, Ruby etc. from India were used for inlay work. White Marble from Makrana Rajasthan & Red Sand stone from Fatehpur Sikri near Agra were used in construction of Taj Mahal.

VI. Taj Mahal- <u>1878</u>-Frontal View:-

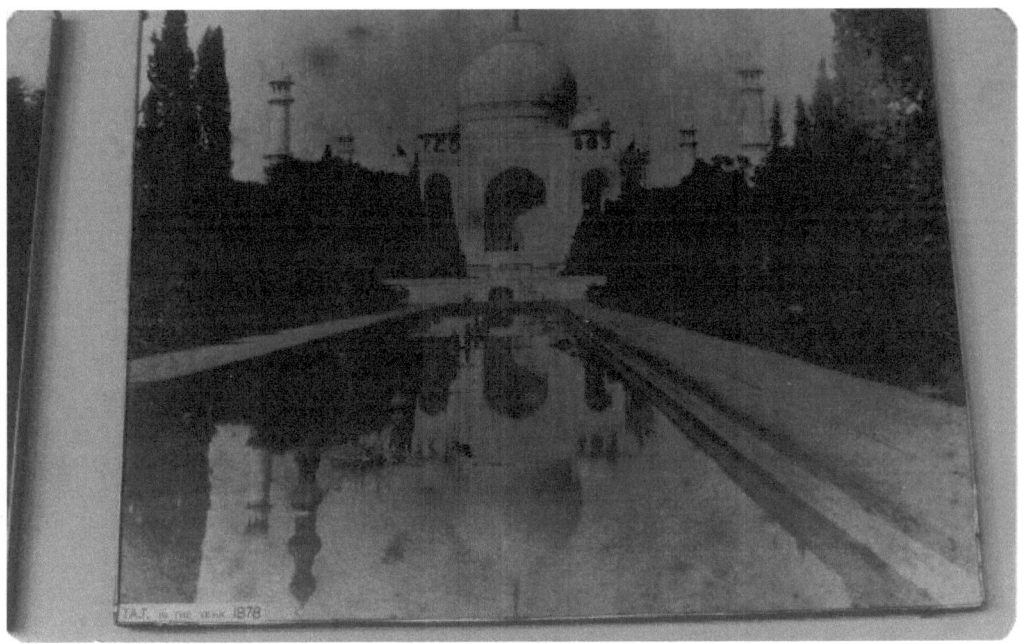

VII. Taj Mahal- <u>1882</u>-Frontal View:-

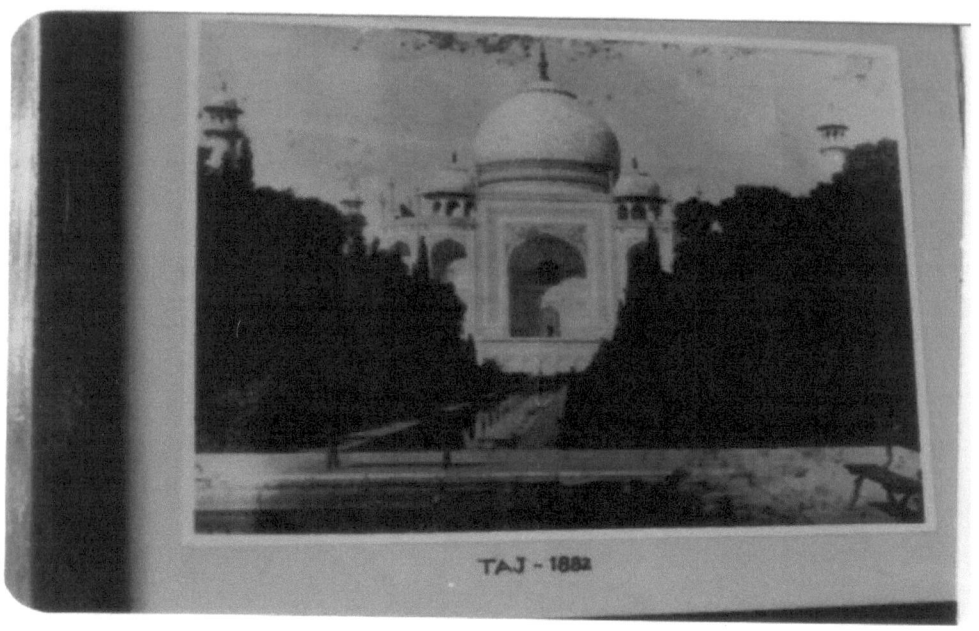

TAJ - 1882

20,000 workers were employed daily, 1000 elephants for building material from all over India & Central Asia. 'Mumtazabad' now 'Tajganj' near Taj Mahal a small town was set up in 4 March 1633 A.D. to accommodate all workers & material.

VIII. Taj Mahal - <u>1884</u> - British Officials in group with big size of tree in back view:-

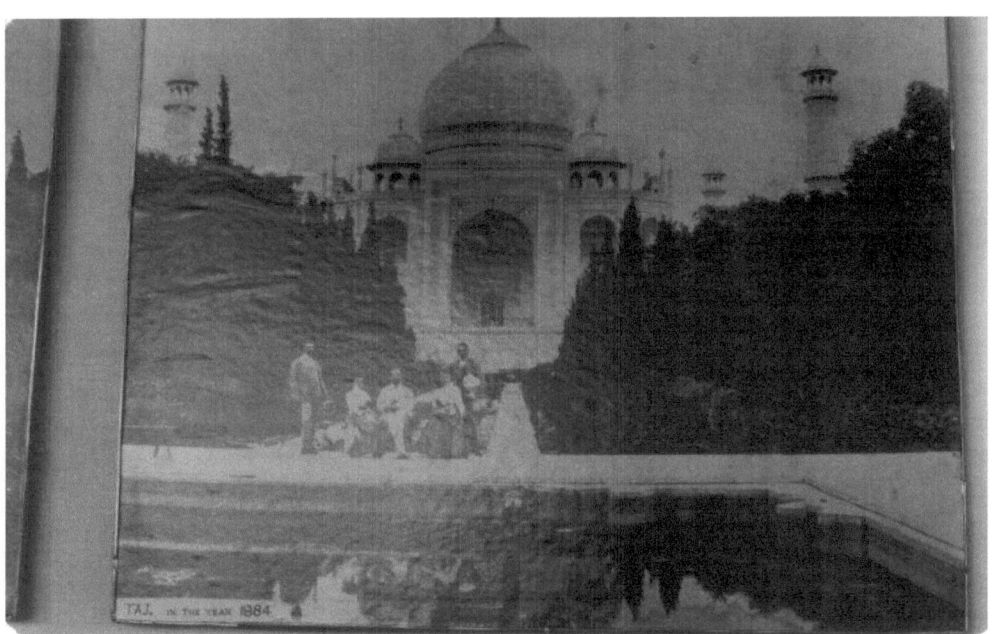

IX. Taj Mahal - <u>1890</u> – Photograph taken by British with big size of tree in view:-

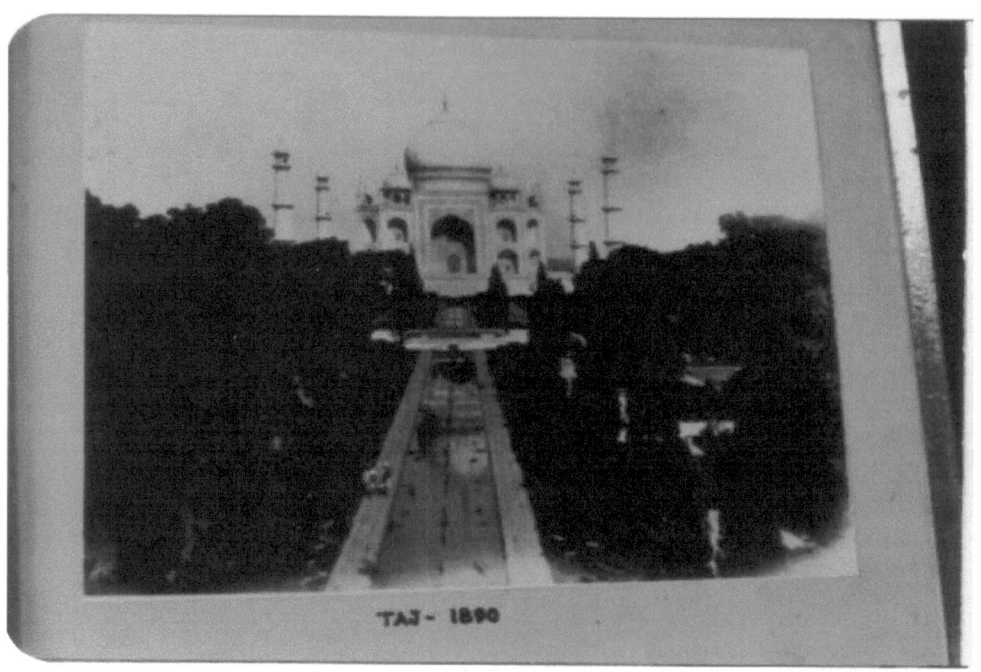

TAJ- 1890

Shah Jahan becomes Emperor in 1628 A.D. He called her Mumtaz Mahal, "Jewel of the Palace."

X. Taj Mahal - <u>1892</u> – Photograph taken by British with big size box Camera covered by black cloth:-

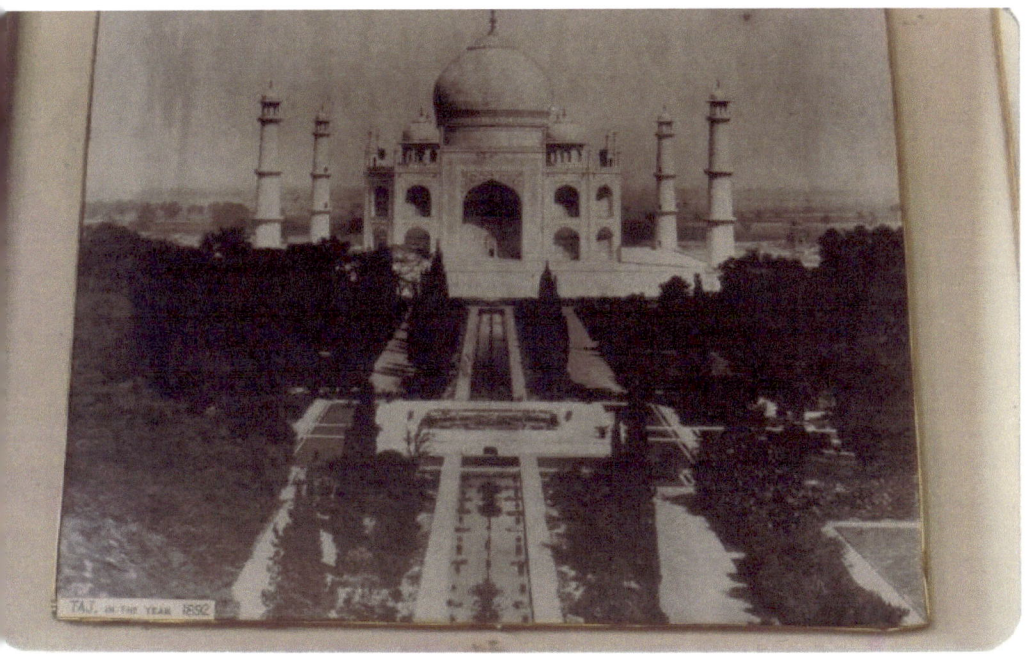

TAJ. IN THE YEAR 1892

She accompanied him on military campaigns, advised him on affairs of state, and was loved by his subjects for her charitable work.

XI. Taj Mahal - <u>1892</u> – Photograph taken by British with big size box Camera covered by black cloth:-

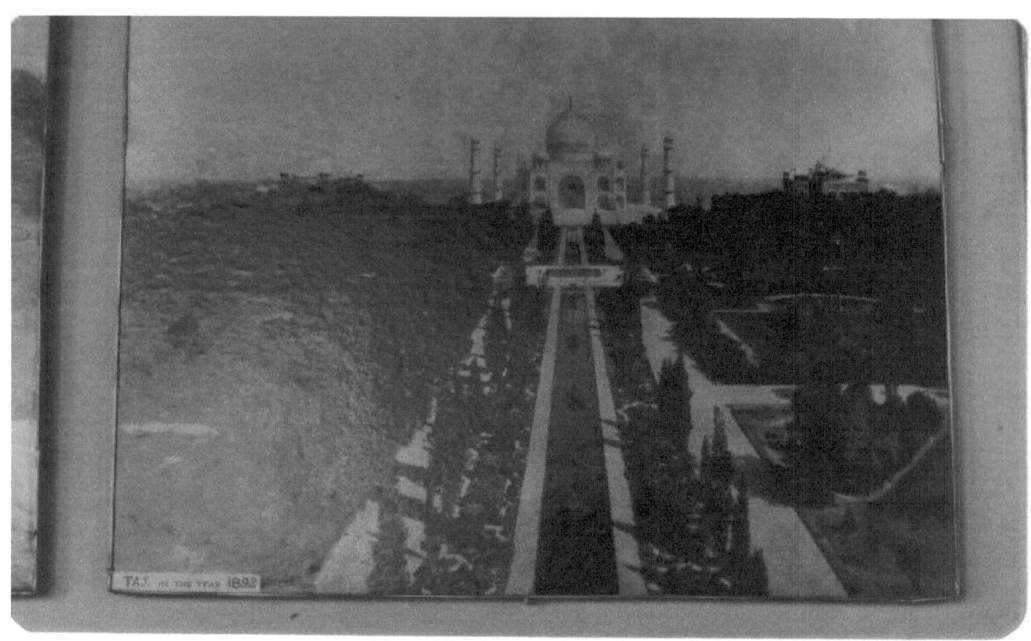

In 1631, Mumtaz Mahal died giving birth to their 14th child.

XII. Taj Mahal - <u>1893</u> – Photograph taken by British with big size box Camera covered by black cloth:-

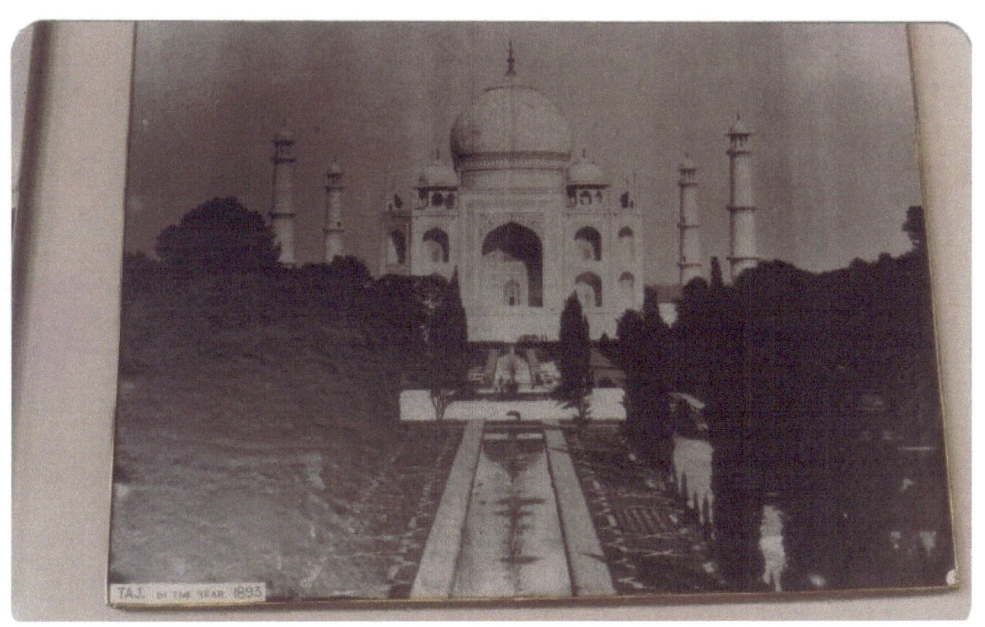

TAJ, IN THE YEAR 1893

In 8 January 1632 Body of Mumtaj Mahal reburied at Agra. Mughal Emperor Shaha Jahan decided to raise a memorial to his beloved queen Mumtaj Mahal, Shah Jahan sent for a council of architects & expressed his desire to build a memorial 'nayab' (unrivalled, unique), 'kamal' (miraculous), 'lateef' (beautiful) and 'ajeebo-gharib (wonderful) mausoleum Taj Mahal Construction Period: 1631-1648 A.D.-Total time taken-17 years.

XIII. Taj Mahal - <u>1894</u> – Photograph taken by British with big size box Camera covered by black cloth:-

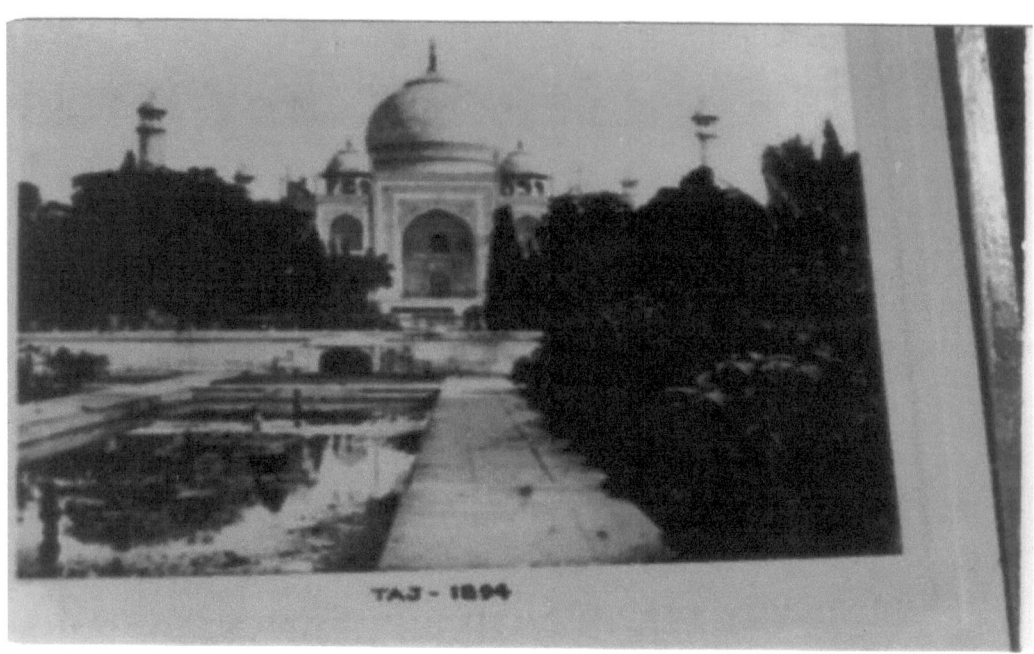

TAJ - 1894

In 28 December 1633 Shah Jahan issued a Farman to Raja jai Singh for awarding exchange properties of Taj Mahal

XIII. Taj Mahal - <u>1901</u> – Photograph taken by British:-

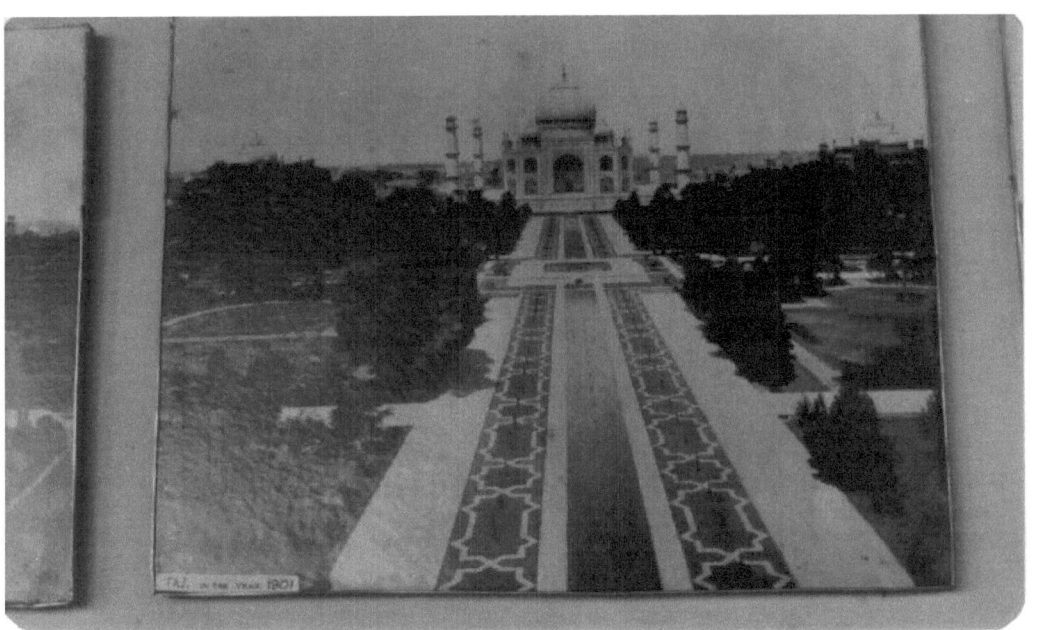

In 1657 Shah Jahan fell ill, and in 1658 his son Aurangzeb took the opportunity to imprison his father and seize the throne. Shah Jahan remained in captivity until his death in 31 January 1666.

XIV. Taj Mahal - <u>1910</u> – Photograph taken when Care taking started by British:-

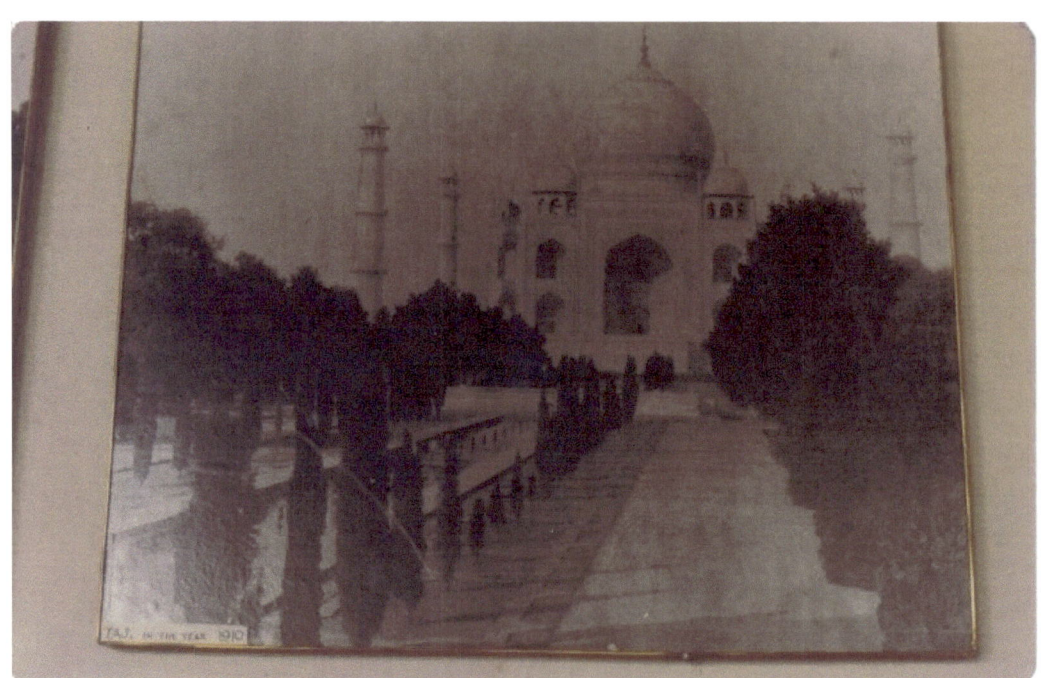

In 31 January 1666 Death & burial of Emperor Shah Jahan.

XV. Taj Mahal - <u>1910</u> – Photograph taken when Care taking started by British:-

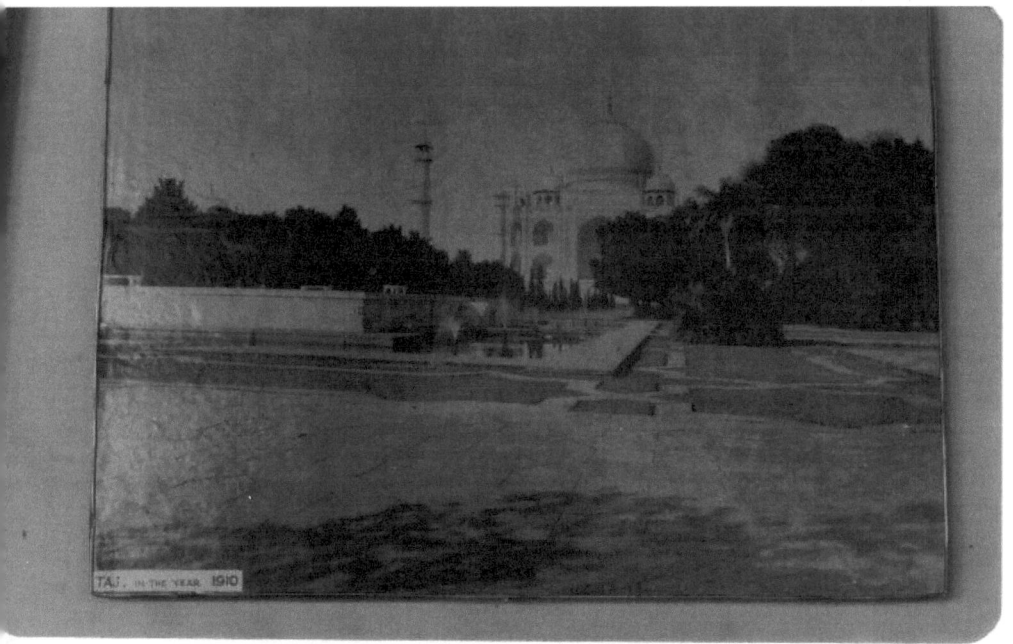

The massive silver doors of the Taj Mahal costing Lacks of rupees were taken away by Jat's during weakening of massive Mughal power when they captured the Agra city after the death of Aurangzeb.

XVI. Taj Mahal - <u>1914</u> – Circular Garden- Photograph taken when Care taking started by British:-

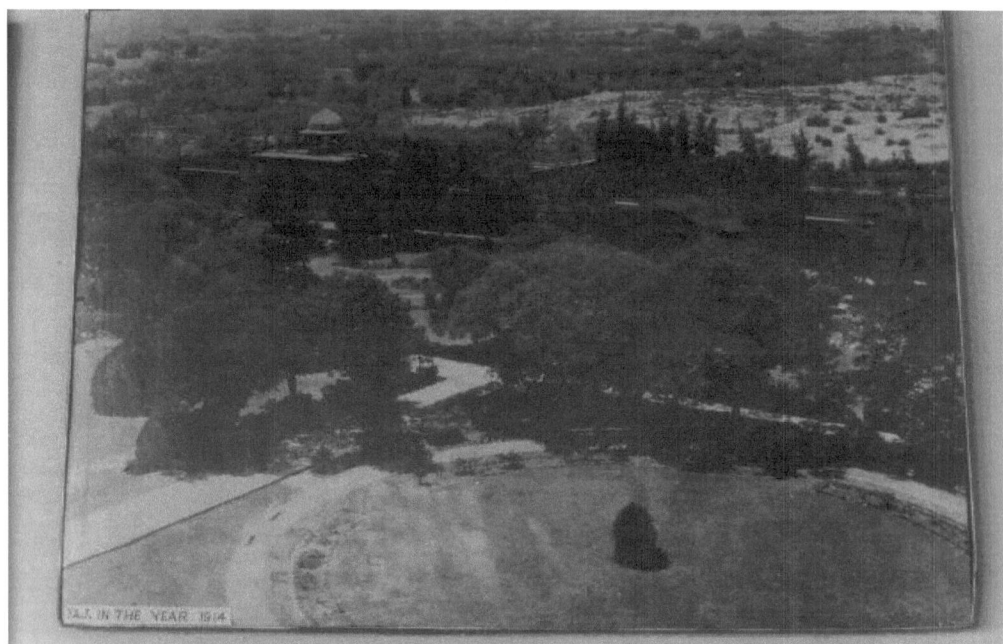

Now days this circular designed garden is not in Taj Mahal, It is converted in simple garden based on Symmetrical *Charbagh* pattern of all Mughal Gardens.

XVII. Taj Mahal - <u>1914</u> – Circular Garden- Photograph taken when Care taking started by British:-

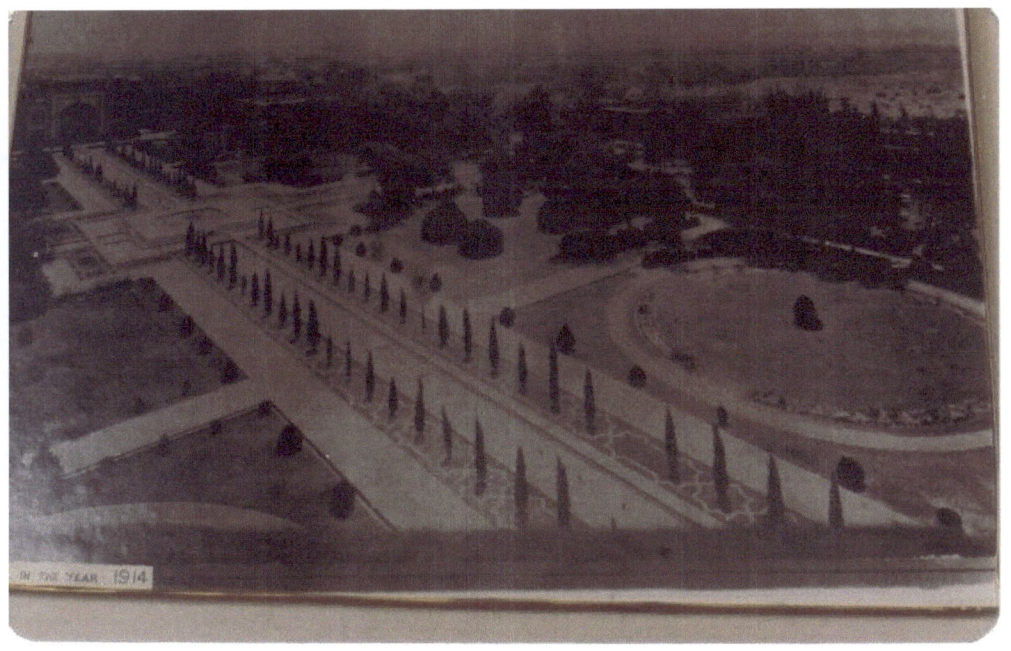

Now days this circular designed garden is not in Taj Mahal, It is converted in simple garden based on Symmetrical *Charbagh* pattern of all Mughal Gardens.

XVIII. Taj Mahal - <u>1914</u> – Circular Garden- Photograph taken when Care taking started by British:-

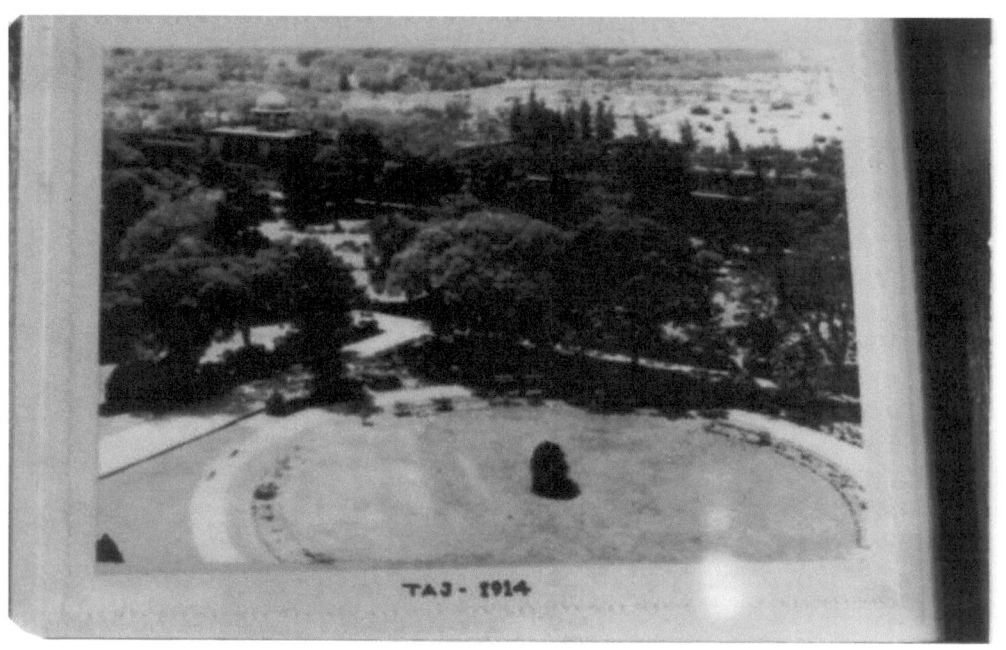

TAJ - 1914

Now days this circular designed garden is not in Taj Mahal, It is converted in simple garden based on Symmetrical *Charbagh* pattern of all Mughal Gardens.

XIX. Taj Mahal - <u>1950</u> - Photograph taken when Care taking started in full swing after independence:-

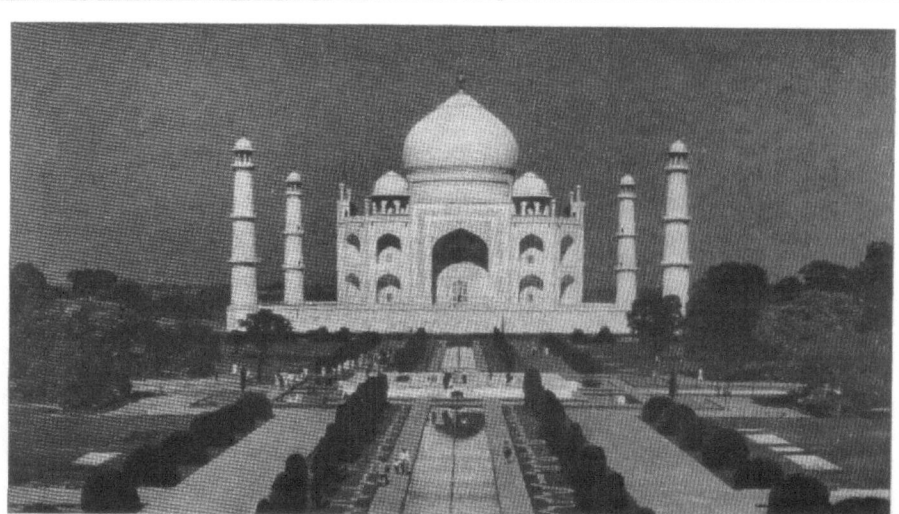

Taj in 1950

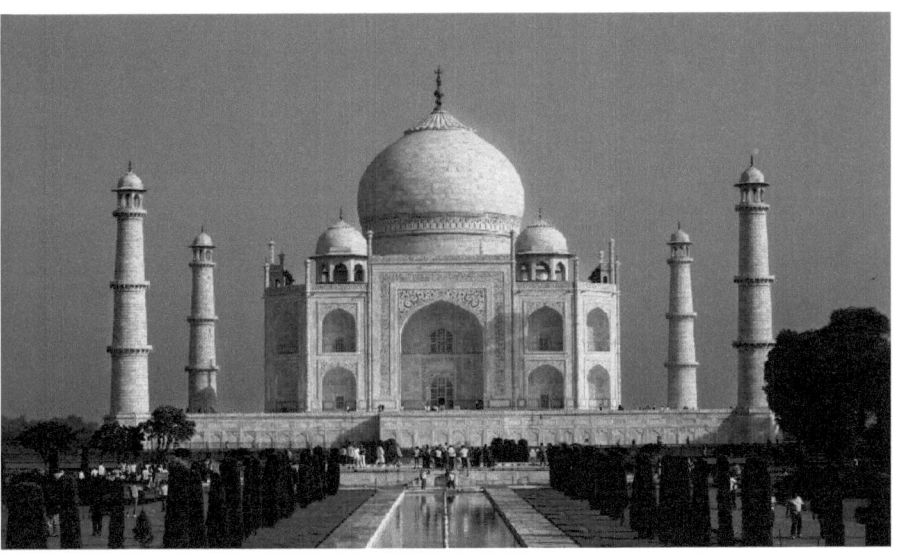

Total area of Taj Mahal Complex is 579.2m x304.8 mt. (Taj -1950)

XX. Taj Mahal - <u>1964</u> –

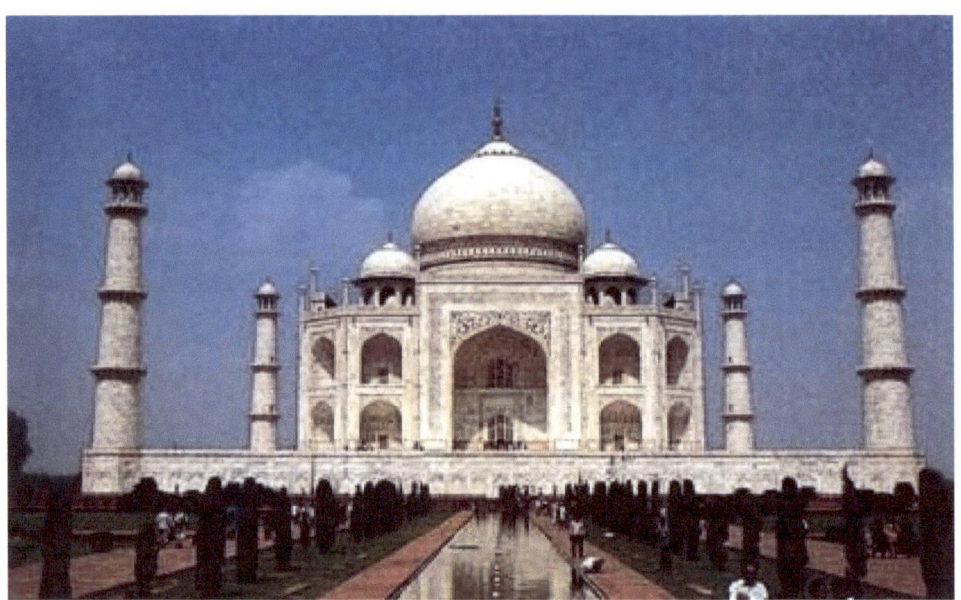

Total weight of the dome is 12,192.56 tones & Total Height of the Taj Mahal is243'-6'' (up to the finial){187'+32'-51/2''+19+4}

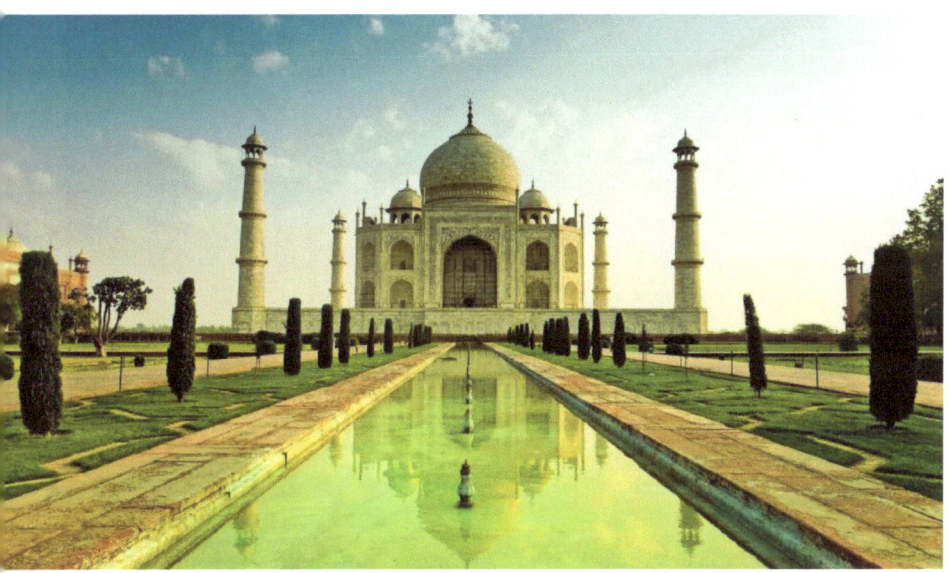

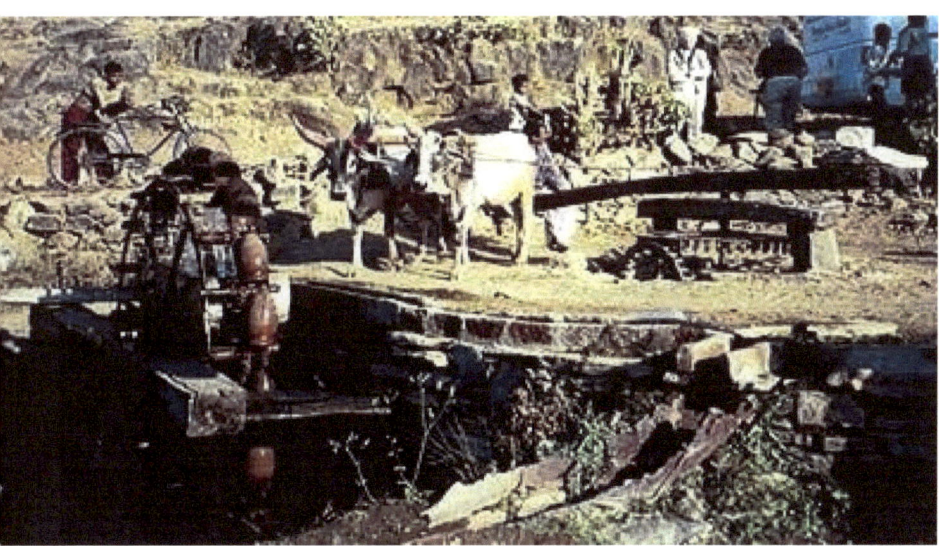

Water system in fountains & for gardens from Yamuna river in back by Persian wheel system
'Rahat': **The Giant Wheel system pulled by Animals-bulls, Horses, which lift water from Yamuna river lower level of to upper level of Taj Mahal)**

Topic 4:- Taj Mahal-Three Dimensional (3D) View:-

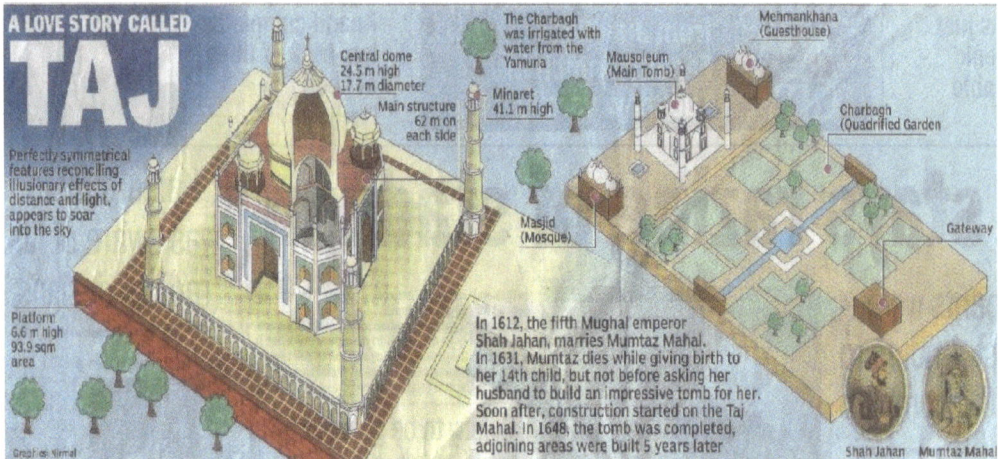

Taj Mahal-Three Dimensional (3D) View showing all four direction buildings including Mosque, *Mahmankhana*-Guest house, Big Entry Gate & Quadrified symmetrical *Cahrbagh* (Four Gardens) & water Channels with fountains system.

Topic 5:- Construction of the Taj Mahal:-

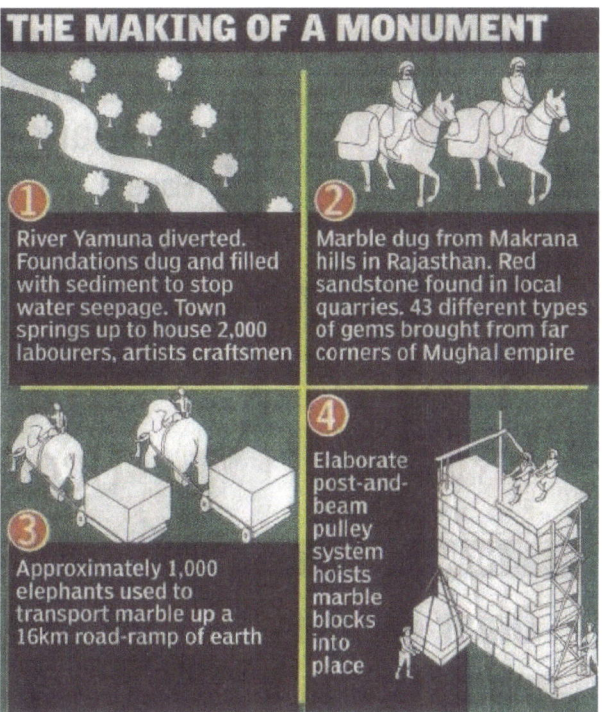

THE MAKING OF A MONUMENT

1 River Yamuna diverted. Foundations dug and filled with sediment to stop water seepage. Town springs up to house 2,000 labourers, artists craftsmen

2 Marble dug from Makrana hills in Rajasthan. Red sandstone found in local quarries. 43 different types of gems brought from far corners of Mughal empire

3 Approximately 1,000 elephants used to transport marble up a 16km road-ramp of earth

4 Elaborate post-and-beam pulley system hoists marble blocks into place

Construction of Taj Mahal during Medieval Time 450 years back is massive Art & hard work taken by Emperor Shah Jahan through more than 20 Thousand skilled & non skilled workers Day & Night under his supervision personally & employed many supervisors under Chief Architect & designers of Taj Mahal. Massive Work taken through with local, outside worker even outside, Countries like Persia & Samarkand etc. Thousand of Horses, Ass, Elephants & Camel were deployed for extensive hard work of carrying the building material like heavy white marble stones from Makrana in Rajasthan through Bullock Carts, Horse Carts & other means of Available transport of that time from one city to another Taj Mahal site Agra City. Red Sand Stone from local areas & 43 type of all different color Gem stones precious & semi precious stones were brought from different countries for intricate caving work, calligraphic work like black Holy Quran letters in white Marble & flower designs etc. Beam Pulley system was used to place marble blocks on right place. There is one Myth about that Emperor Shah Jahan cut workers hands just after the contraction of Taj Mahal, but it is not true. He only suggested to his workers even requested after giving them huge amount of Gold & Silver as their reward for not to built same Taj Mahal like any structure or look alike or same building any where due to making Taj Mahal for its Uniqueness in the World.

Topic 6:- Taj Mahal-The interior water well (Work as real Taj Mahal foundation):-

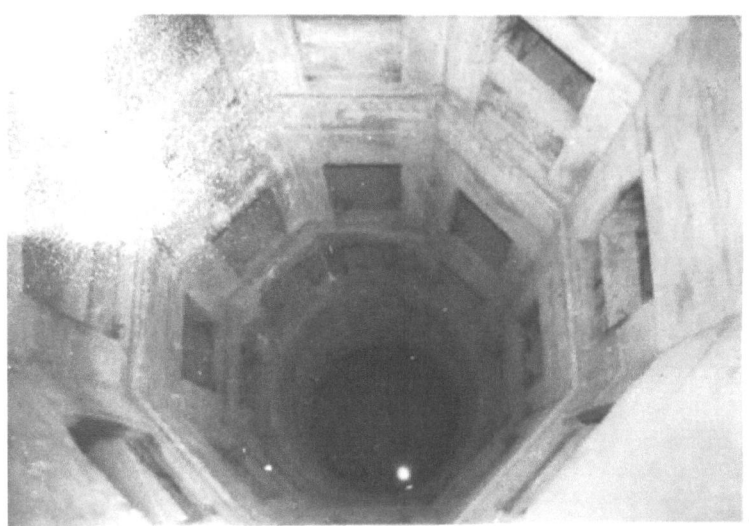

Now days it is covered & Not open for Public.
Taj Mahal foundation is based on strong walled Deep dry wells of Lakhauri bricks, lime mortar & Rubble inside & stone masonry outside which supports entire weight of Taj Mahal along with safety from earth quake jurks & subsoil water level of Yamuna river which flows just behind to the Taj Mahal. Base of plastering Cement was prepared by naturally available Tree Gums, lentils along with several hours baked small bricks called Lahauri bricks or *kakaiya Eeet.*

Shahajahan's Farmans (Orders) for Taj Mahal

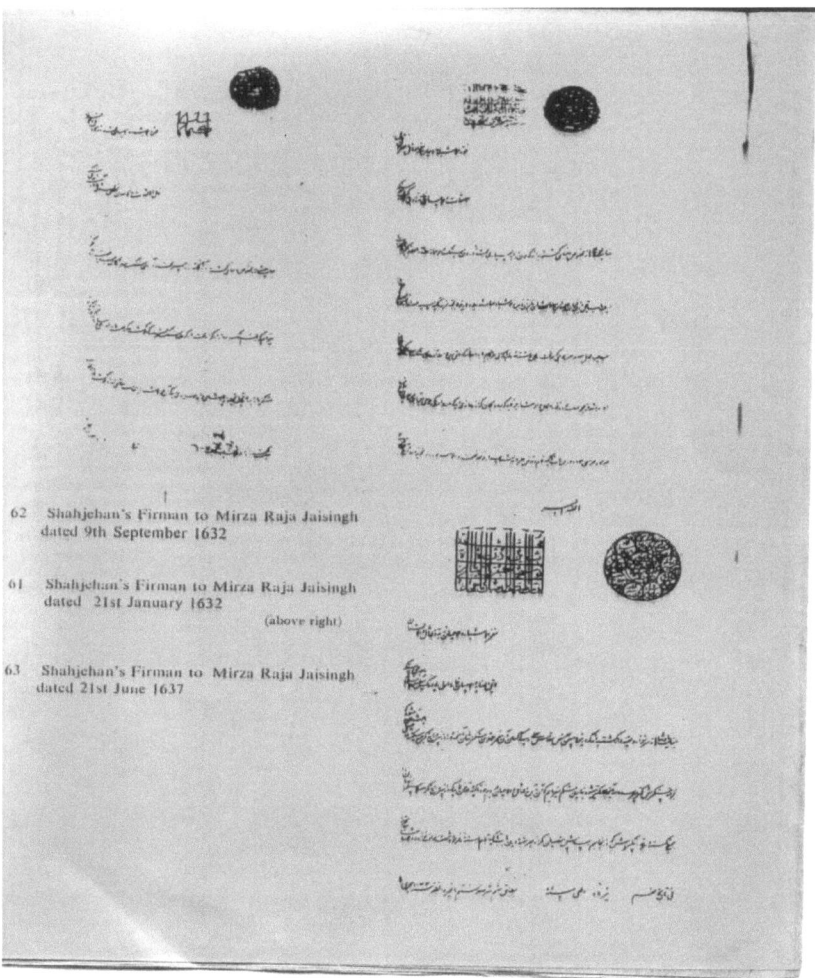

62   Shahjehan's Firman to Mirza Raja Jaisingh
      dated 9th September 1632

61   Shahjehan's Firman to Mirza Raja Jaisingh
      dated 21st January 1632
                                        (above right)

63   Shahjehan's Firman to Mirza Raja Jaisingh
      dated 21st June 1637

Shaha Jahan's *Farmans* (Royal Orders) for Taj Mahal to Mirza Raja Jai Singh dated 9th September 1632, 21st January 1632 & 21st June 1637 for construction, Bringing Marble from Makrana-Rajsthan etc.

Emperor Shah Jahan's Signature on Farman:-

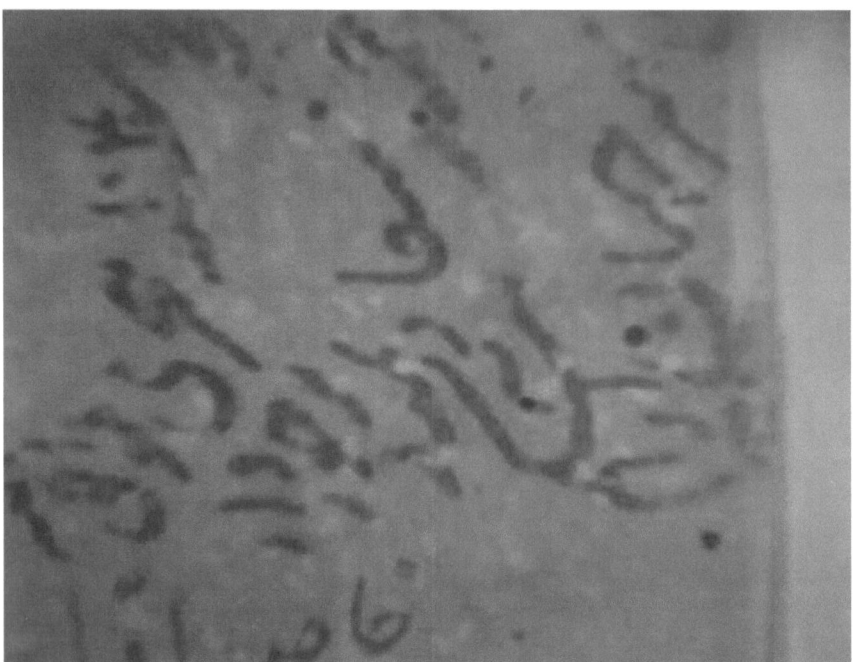

Photograph taken from Raja Library Farman Collection Rampur U.P.

Shah Jahan's Royal Seal on Farman

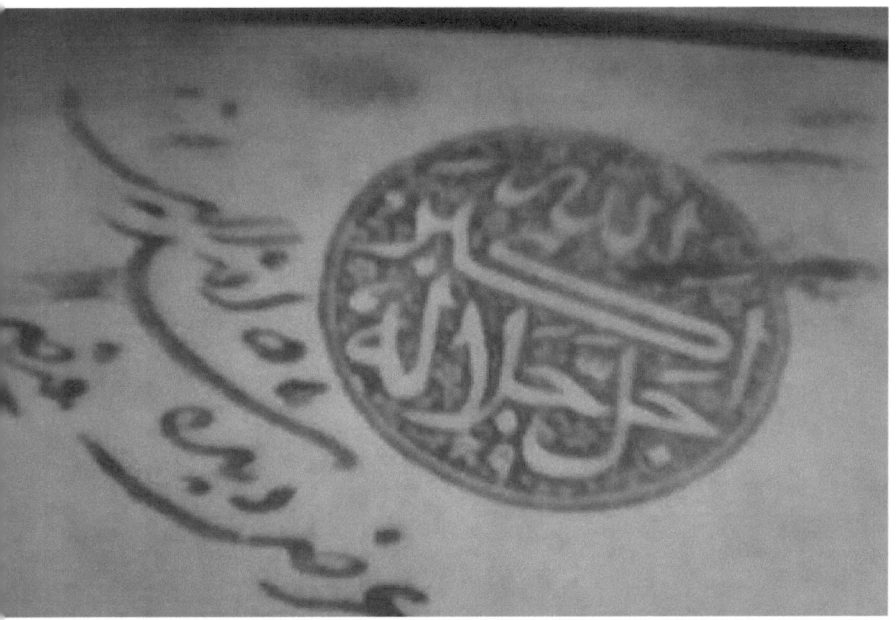

Photograph taken from Raja Library Farman Collection Rampur U.P

Marriage of Shah Jahan to Mumtaj Mahal (Arjumand Banu Begum)   took place in 1612 on 10 May

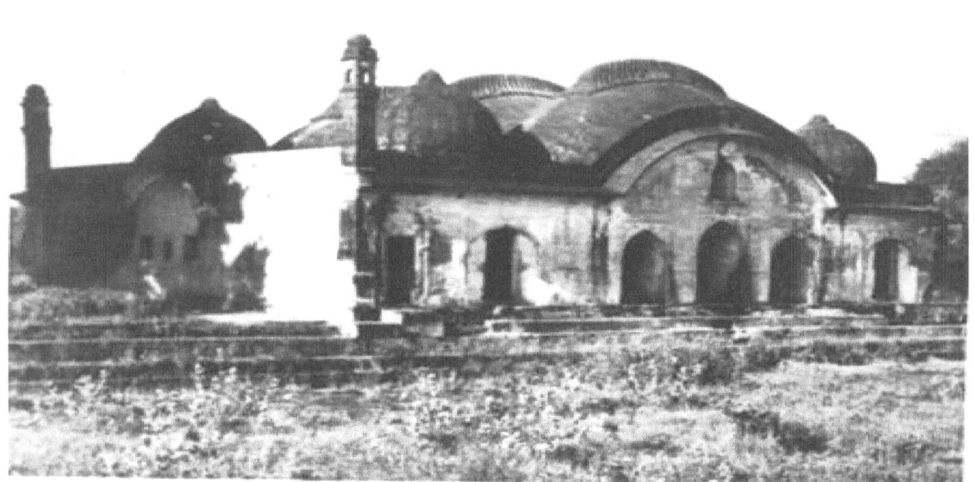

Palace in Barhanpur where Mumtaz Mahal died

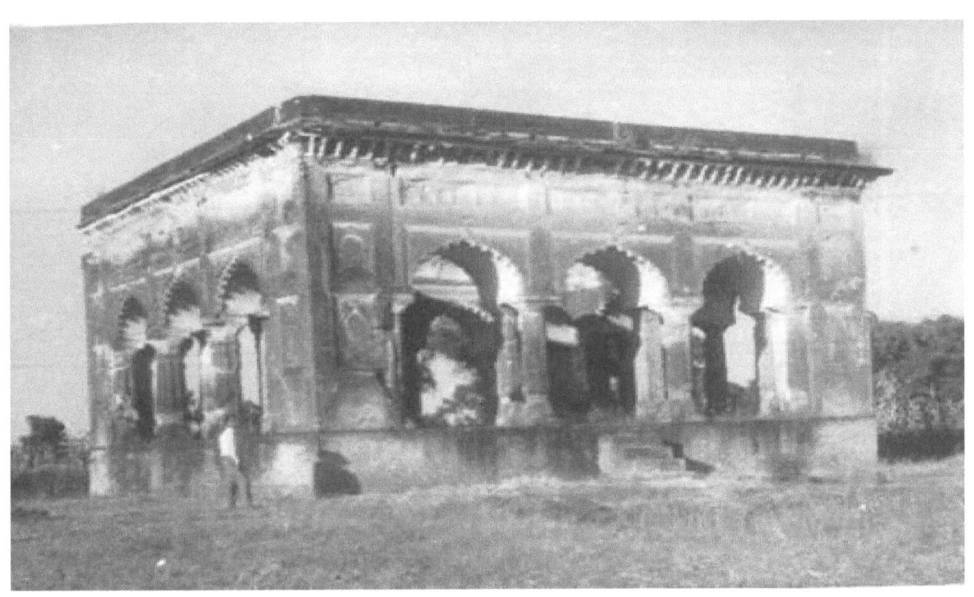

Barhanpur Pavilion where Mumtaz is said to be buried

In11 December, 1631, Body of Mumtaj Mahal taken from Burhanpur to Taj Mahal Agra

View of sealed doors & windows in back

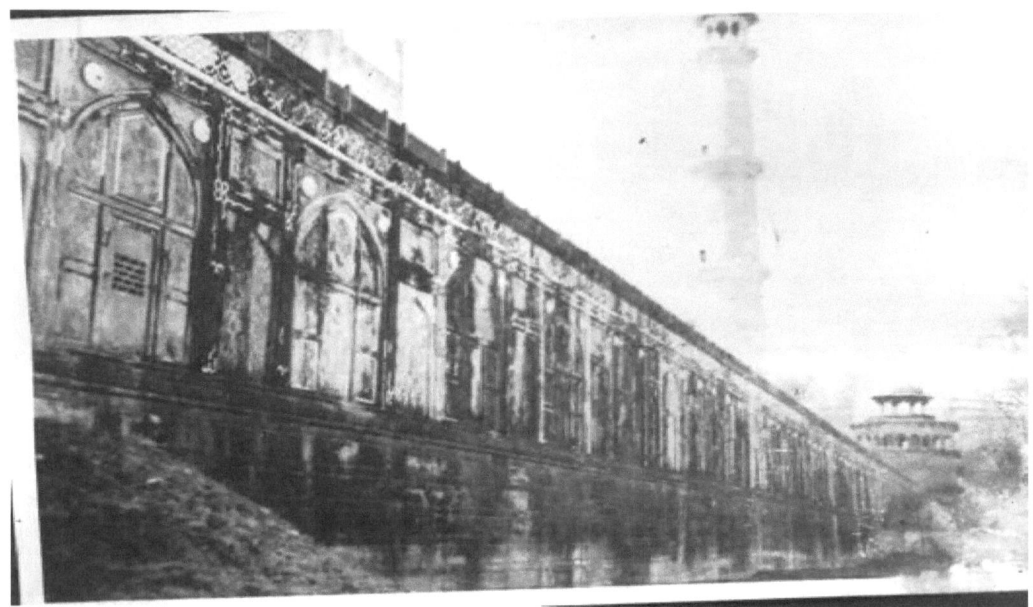

Now days these doors are covered & Not open for public

Taj Mahal-Staircase that leads to the lower levels

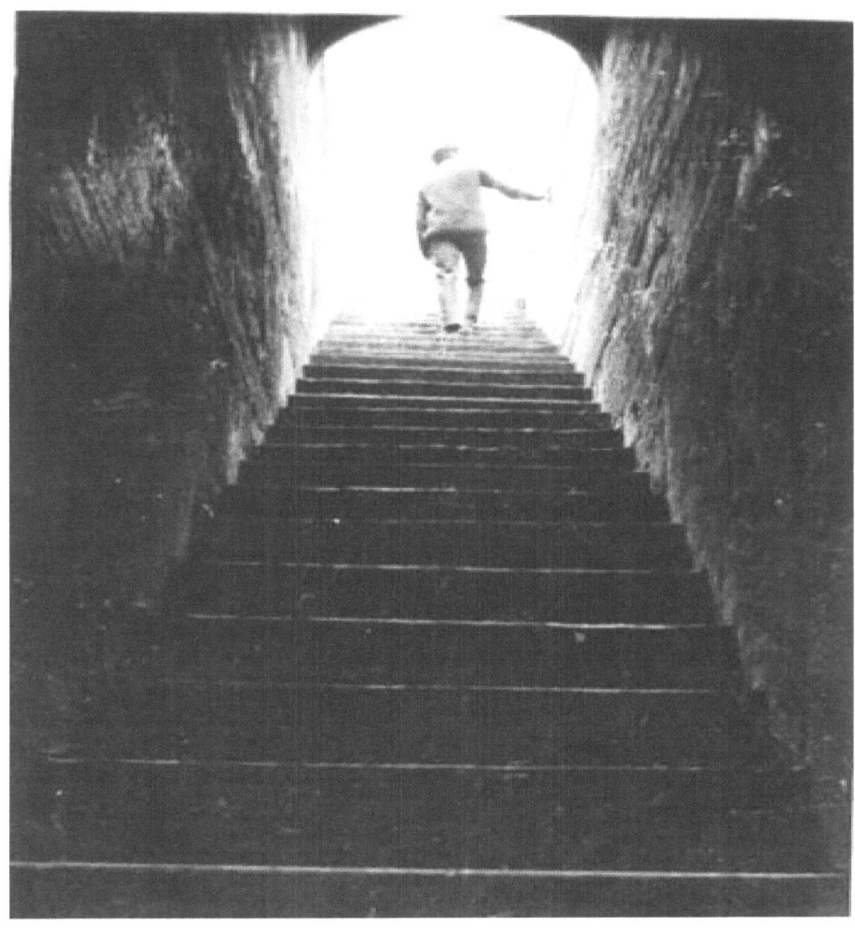

Now days it is covered & Not open for public

Taj Mahal-One of the 22 rooms in the secret lower level

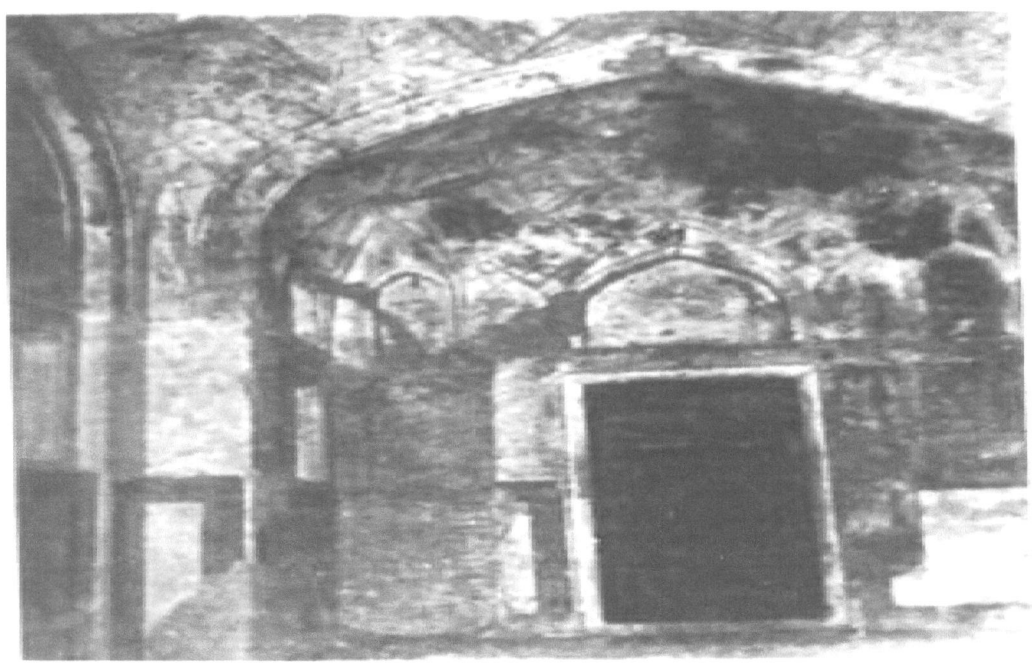

Now days it is covered & Not open for public

Taj Mahal-Interior of one of the 22 Secret Rooms

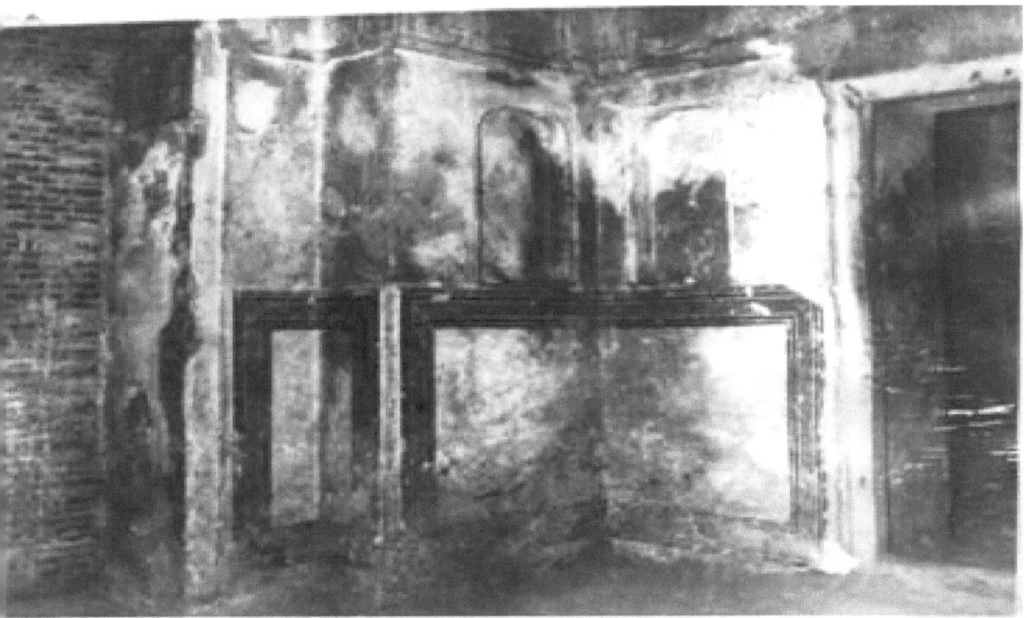

Now days it is covered & Not open for public

Taj Mahal Huge ventilator sealed shut with bricks

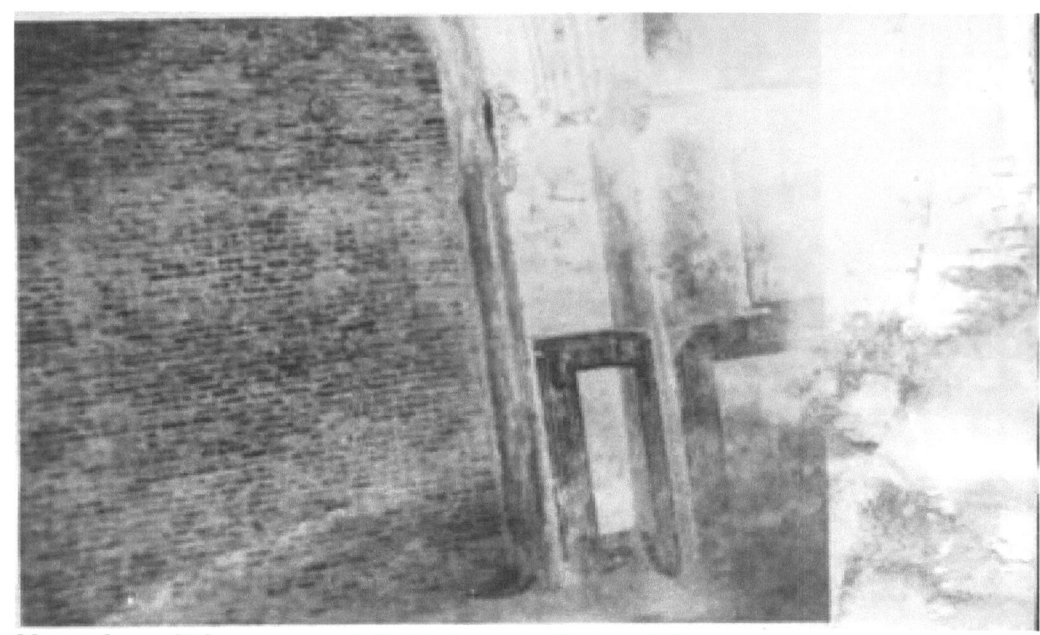

Now days it is covered & Not open for public

Taj Mahal-Interior of another of the locked Rooms

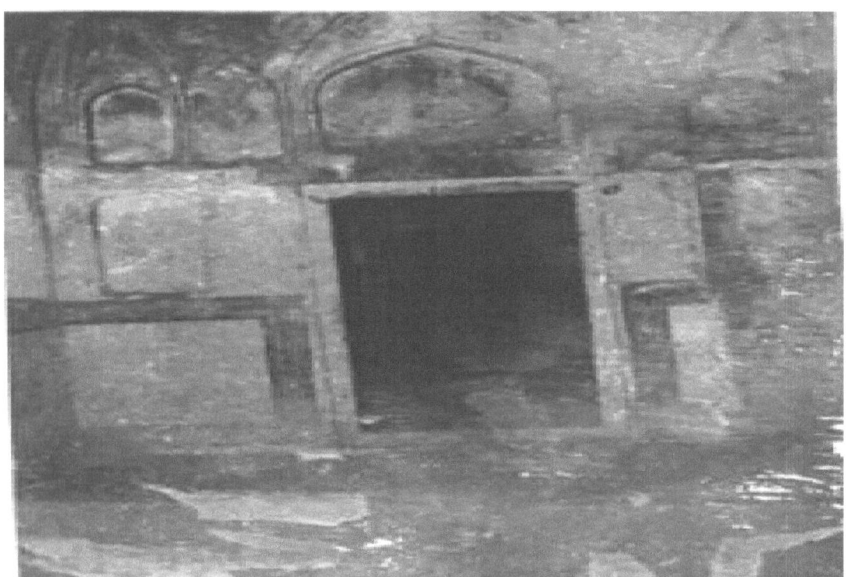

Now days it is covered & Not open for public

Taj Mahal-Secret bricked door that hides more evidence

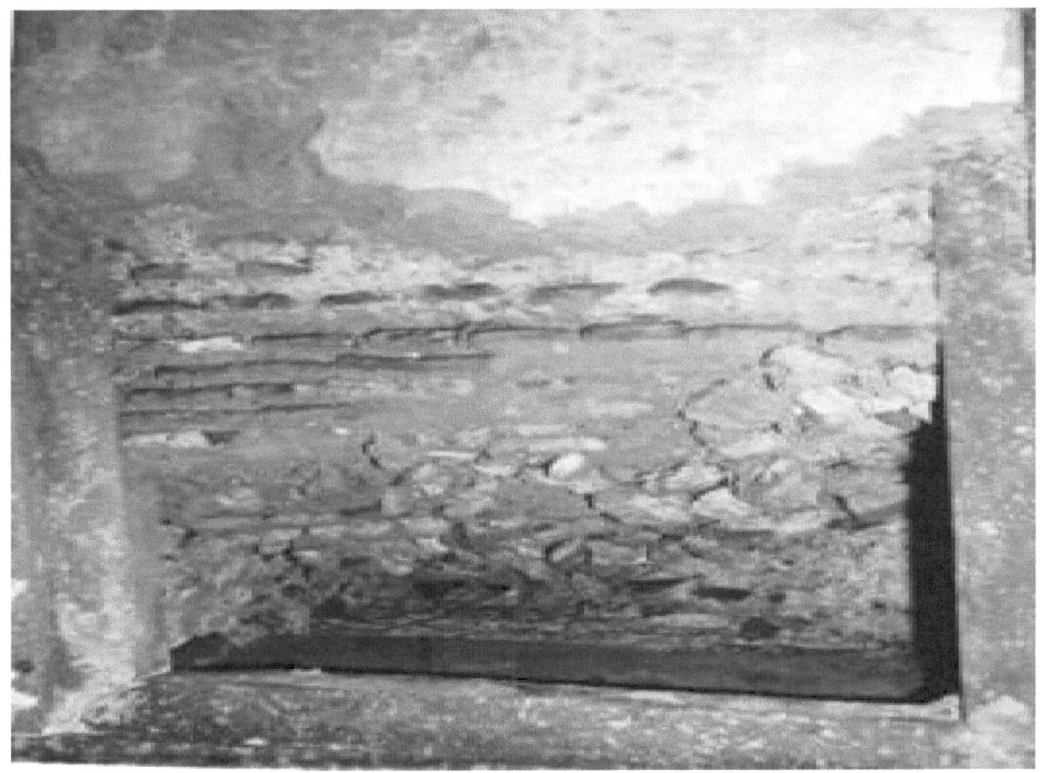

Now days it is covered & Not open for public

Taj Mahal-Secret walled door that leads to other Rooms

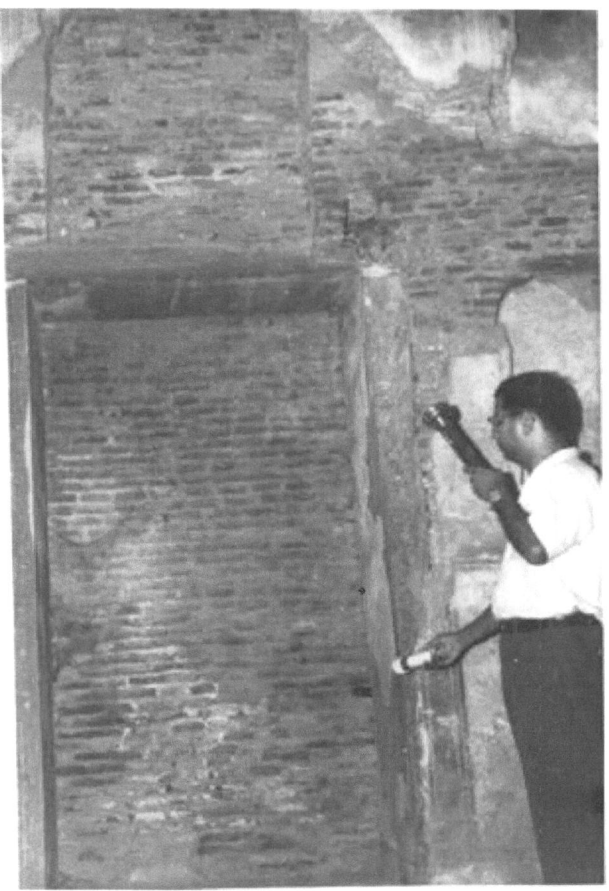

Now days it is covered & Not open for public

Topic 7:- Muslim & Mughal (Indo- Islamic or Indo-Sarsenic Style) Architecture:-

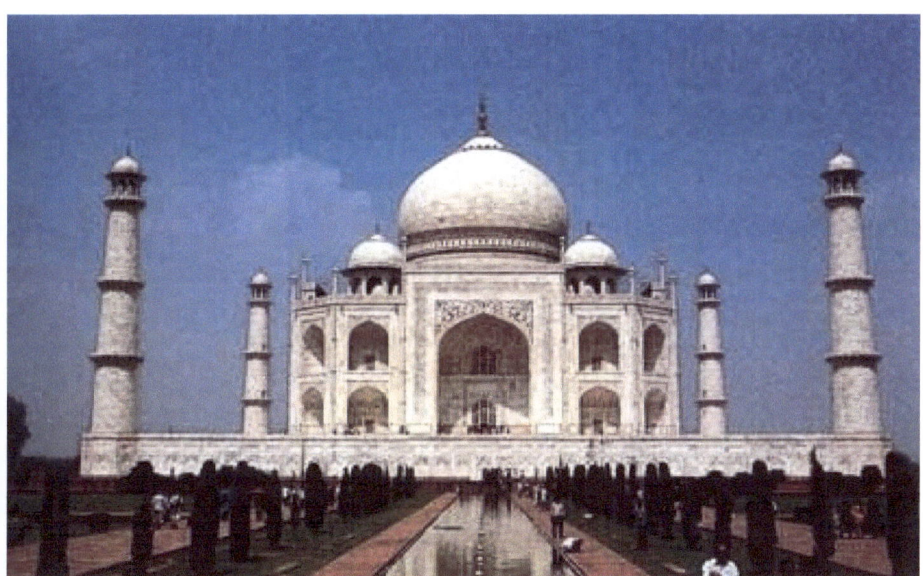

Now days Taj Mahal- Presently seven wonders of the World, (World Heritage Site):-

In 1191, the first of many dynasties ruled by Islamic sultans captured Delhi and made it a power base for governing northern India. To celebrate the triumph of Islam, these sultans created an impressive complex of buildings outside Delhi, including a mosque with a very tall minaret (tower). Hindu buildings reflected nature in both their shapes and decorations, but Islamic artists and architects were prohibited from using images, even though floral decoration was sometimes allowed. Instead they worked in pure geometric designs, reflecting the abstract definition of Allah.

The purity of the decoration on the Qutb Minar is a fine example of this art. In the domain of architecture the Mughals made their remarkable contribution to Indian culture. The simplicity of the pre-Mughal architecture gave place to the delicate ornamental style of the Mughals. The Mughal architecture blended the Persian and Indian styles. Graceful domes, cupolas at the corners standing on pillars, a huge palace hall and vaulted gateway are some of the salient features of the Mughal architecture. The new style of building mausoleums in the middle of park-like enclosures and double domes was introduced by the Mughals.

Buildings constructed during the reigns of Babur and Humayun, under the influence of Persian architecture were mostly unimpressed. Out of the structures built by Babur, only the mosque in Kabuli Bagh at Panipat and the Jama Masjid at Sambhal exist today. Sher Shah completed the the construction of Purana Qila at Delhi. The mosque in the Purana Qila known as Qila-i-Kuhana Masjid is admired by many today. Sher Shah's tomb which was built by himself at Sasaram in Bihar is one of the best architectural monuments in India. Mughal architecture had a new impetus in the reign of Akbar. The new style began by Sher Shah was developed by Akbar whose tolerant spirit and artistic sense made a synthesis of the Persian and Indian styles in architecture.

From the 1500's, the Mughal emperors continued to build, not only in Delhi but also in other capitals such as Agra and Lahore. In 1571, the emperor Akbar ordered the building of a completely new city called Fatehpur Sikri, near Agra. This city, an offering of thanksgiving by Akbar for the gift of sons who would carry on his line, was abandoned soon after it was built. It remains a perfect example of a Mughal city. It contains buildings constructed, like the Qutb Minar, of red sandstone. Because Akbar was anxious to promote cooperation between Muslims and Hindus, he allowed his Hindu stonemasons to embellish the buildings at Fatehpur Sikri with decorations that might have graced a Hindu palace. Akbar ordered the building of several forts in defence of his major cities. His builders again used red sandstone for these stout buildings.

The red forts, like other buildings completed at the same time and made of the same material, have a heavy appearance. They take their colour from the Indian countryside and rise from the landscape like rocks and hills. India's hot climate often influenced its architectural planning. The best-known building in Fatehpur Sikri is a five-storey pavilion with no walls. Only rows of pillars hold up the roof of one storey which becomes the floor of the one above. On the terraces of this pavilion, the emperor and his ladies could enjoy the views, shelter from the sun, and take advantage of cooling breezes. Garden design also owed much to the Indian climate. The emperor and his court spent much of the year in Kashmir, where people lived outdoors.

The gardens of the emperor and his nobles had terraces and stairways with streams running alongside them carrying cool water down from the mountains to nearby lakes. There was also a complex system of fountains and cascades. At Delhi and Agra, special channels carried cooling water through the interiors of buildings. In the 1600's, Akbar's grandson, the emperor Shah Jahan, built mosques and other buildings within the Red Forts of Delhi and Agra. These buildings were made of glistening white marble. So too was the magnificent Taj Mahal, the tomb that Shah Jahan ordered for his wife beside the Jamuna River, at Agra.

The Mughals made their remarkable contribution of architecture in Indian culture. The simplicity of the pre-Mughal architecture gave place to the delicate ornamental style of the Mughals. The Mughal architecture blended the Persian and Indian styles. Graceful domes, cupolas at the corners standing on pillars, a huge palace hall and vaulted gateway are some of the salient features of the Mughal architecture. The new style of building mausoleums in the middle of park-like enclosures and double domes was introduced by the Mughals.

Topic 8:- Story of World Fame Taj Mahal of Agra: -

The **Taj Mahal (Crown Palace),** often called the most beautiful building in the world, was built by an emperor as a memorial to his beloved wife.

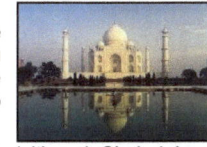

Prince Khurram, the future Shah Jahan, was born in 1592. His father was Jahangir, the fourth Mughal emperor of India. According to legend, the prince met **Arjumand Banu Begum,** the daughter of his father's prime minister, at a bazaar when he was 14 and she was 15. Smitten, the prince bought a diamond from the girl for 10,000 rupees, then went to his father and announced his desire to marry her.

Their **wedding took place five years later, in 1612.** From that time they were inseparable (although Shah Jahan also had other wives). **After becoming Emperor in 1628, Shah Jahan entrusted Arjumand Banu with the royal seal. He called her Mumtaz Mahal, "jewel of the palace." She accompanied him on military campaigns, advised him on affairs of state, and was loved by his subjects for her charitable work.**

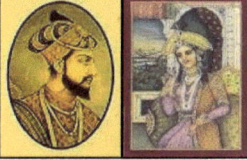

In 1631, Mumtaz Mahal died giving birth to their 14th child. Her heartbroken husband spent approximately two decades, and much of the money in the royal treasury, fulfilling his wife's dying wish by building a monument to their love.

Mughal Emperor Shaha Jahan decided to raise a memorial to his beloved Queen Mumtaj Mahal, Shah Jahan sent for a council of architects & expressed his desire to build a memorial 'nayab' (unrivalled, unique), 'kamal' (miraculous), 'lateef' (beautiful) and 'ajeebo-gharib (wonderful) mausoleum, which would suppress every other building in the world and no other monument would ever rival it in grandeur & magnificence. Various architects submitted designs of the proposed tomb on paper. One was selected by the Emperor-Shah Jahan; according to this a model was prepared in wood. The unique proportions of the Taj Mahal were evolved on a wooden model and, as seems certain, many wooden models were prepared which helped to give the perfect design. This final design was ultimately translated into stone in actual size.

This is how the conception of a wonderful memorial was presented in its finest & most beautiful expression.

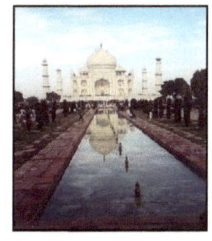

The Taj Mahal is considered one of the wonders of the world. It stands amid acres of gardens on the banks of the Yamuna River in Agra. The most famous part of the monument is the tomb of Mumtaz Mahal with its white marble dome, but the 42-acre complex also includes mosques, minarets and other buildings.

In 1657 Shah Jahan fell ill, and in 1658 his son Aurangzeb took the opportunity to imprison his father and seize the throne. Shah Jahan remained in captivity until his death in 31st. January 1666. It is said he spent the last days of his life staring into a small piece of glass at the reflection of the Taj Mahal, and died with the mirror in his hand. He is buried in the Taj Mahal with the wife he never forgot. It has been suggested that Shah Jahan never intended to be entombed with his wife, but planned to build a second, black marble Taj to serve as his mausoleum. However, many scholars doubt this story and believe the emperor did indeed wish to be buried near Mumtaz Mahal.

The massive silver doors of the Taj Mahal costing Lacs of rupees were taken away by Jat's during weakening of massive Mughal power when they captured the Agra city after the death of Aurangzeb. In1803 Agra passed into the handsof Britishers, during the rule of East India Company, no attention was paid towards the improvement of Agra city and its historical buildings. During the days of William Bentinck the Taj was on the point of being demolished for the value of its marbles. He also auctioned the marbles in Shah Jahan's palace at Agra. When Lord Curzon came to India he found Agra and its buildings in very deplorable conditions. He spent between 40 to 50 thousand pounds sterling upon the repairs, preservation, conservation & Restoration works.

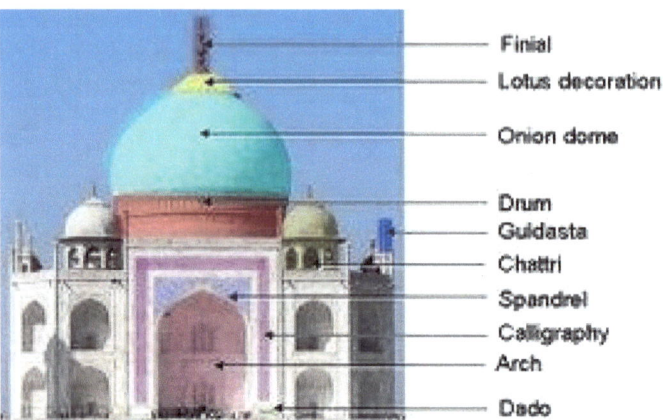

Finial
Lotus decoration
Onion dome
Drum
Guldasta
Chattri
Spandrel
Calligraphy
Arch
Dado

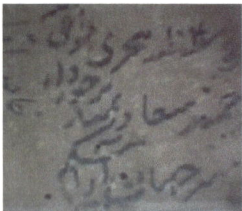

Signature of Shah Jahan in Farman of Marble delivery for Taj Mahal

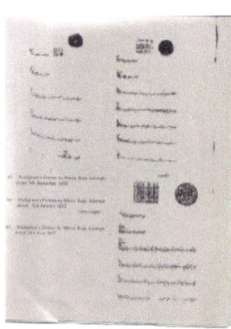

Shaha jahan's Farmans (Royal Orders) for Taj Mahal

The foundation was laid in the subsoil water level with stone-in-limke masonry below the ground and brick-in-lime above. Because of its proximity to the river and the slope of the bank, the entire foundation rest on a compact bed of masonry. At the base on the riverbank side there is a series of deep wells made of rubble-in-lime inside and stone masonry outside. Piers were erected on these walls at close intervals and joined with vaults above. Strong armed laborers dug deep until they reached the water level which extended right down to rock level. They filled the foundations with stone & lime mortar excellently & leveled it with the ground. A series of arches rising above the piers supports the superstructure. **Base of plastering Cement was prepared by naturally available Tree Gums,** lentils along with several hours baked small bricks called **Lahauri bricks or *kakaiya Eeet***.The principles of tension and stress used in the construction are apparent from the compact, arch-supported superstructure and the great overhanging dome.

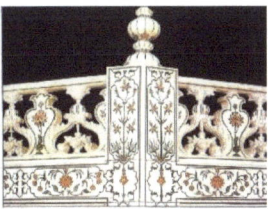

Decorative Carving & Inlay Work on Jali of Taj Mahal.

Salary of 1500/- of those days are equivalent to now days 15 Crore of Rs., To the Engineers, Workers & Artists. There is myths about that Emperor Shaha Jahan had cuted down the workers hand & left them just like the handicaps, but he had taken an Oath & assurence that they will not do this type of same construction work any where for dobling & any Controversy point of view to make Taj Mahal a Unique Architectural wonder. **Total 28 Precious & Semiprecious stones Agate, Coral & Cornelion from Arabia, Diamond from Panna, Jasper from Punjab, jade & Crystals from China, Lapis Lazuli & Sapphire from Srilanka, Neelam, Pearl, Pukhraj, Ruby etc. from India were used for inlay work. White Marble from Makrana Rajasthan & Red Sand stone from Fatehpur Sikri near Agra were used in construction of Taj Mahal. 20,000 workers were employed daily, 1000 elephants for building material from all over India & Central Asia. 'Mumtazabad' now 'Tajganj' near Taj Mahal a small town was set up in 4 March 1633 A.D. to accommodate all workers & material.** Due this reason period of Emperor Shah Jahan is known as 'The Golden Period of Architecture' & Period of Unique White Marble Buildings.

The Third Grave: Basement chambers and a probable Third Grave: -

It is considered that an underground vault exists below the red sandstone platform (chamli-farsh) containing the third and probably the real set of graves. Two staircases on the northern side of the red sandstone plinth of the Taj lead below into basement chambers which are seventeen in number and have laid out in a line on the riverside of a narrow through-corridor. The rooms and corridor are of arcuate construction in brick and plaster, with stucco and painting ornamentation, distributed aesthetically on the soffits. At the extreme points on both sides thrse are doors sunk in the northern wall. As may be surmised; the set on the northern side could have been repeated on all the four sides below the marble structure, with a rotating corridor, chambers and probably a crypt in the center? All being interconnected. This crypt would have contained the third and the real set of graves. The custom of providing cenotaphs or replicas had been followed by the Turks and the Mughals alike as we meet with this practice at the Tomb of Iltutmish at Delhi and at the tombs of Saqtd Khan and Akbar at Agra. The tomb of Akbar has three tombstones, one on the grave and two as cenotaphs.As is generally presumed, the real grave was made underground,in which the dead person could wait till the Day of judgement. The tomb of Itmad-ud-Daulah and Chini-ka-Rauza too had three tombstones each. The lowest of the former was contained in a crypt which was originally accessible from the riverside and has now been completely blocked up.These examples indicate that the Mughals liked to provide three tombstones in a mausoleum.

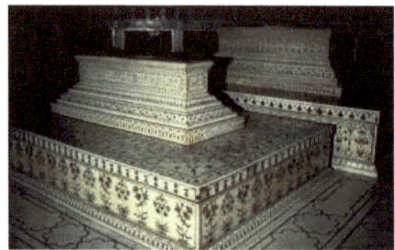

At the Taj, the third is traditionally claimed to exist. It is only in these underground vaults that the third set could have been placed. The doors in the basement corridor no doubt exist and must have originally given entry to some underground arrangement of chambers and corridors. Though they are now blocked, their existence lends weights to the legendary version. At least, we have figures, in the Persian manuscripts which contain the account of 'third grave, expenditure on the Taj Mahal, of costs of three sets of tombstones. While the two are open to us, the third one is still a mystery. It is possible that the crypt and the passages were closed down in 1652 by Aurangzeb to give additional strength to the base which supported such a huge load above.

Topic 9:- Story & Legend of Black Taj Mahal of Shah Jahan:-

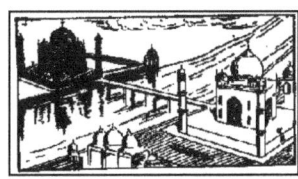

Emperor Shah Jahan according to a popular legend decided to construct another Taj Mahal in black marble on the othe side of the Yamuna River & to connect the two by a gold bridge. This structure was intended to be his own tomb. It has been recorded almost contemporarily by a French merchant Tavernier: "Shaha Jehan began to build his own tomb on the other side of the river but the war with his sons interrupted his plan and Aurangzeb who reign at present is not disposed to complete it." Later gazetteers & guide books mention this story almost invariably. The irregular position of the cenotaph of Shah Jehan as compared to that of Mumtaj Mahal which occupies the center of the hall is said to be proof of this assumption. Particularly Moinuddin attached the greatest credence to the legend & went to the extent of pointing out traces of the unmatured plan on the other side. The Mehtab Burj & the walls which adjoin it opposite the Taj Mahal are generally said to be the foundations & remains of the proposed plan. This has been accepted even in the most recent times. J.B. page spoke of it affirmatively. 'Had the Emperor at first intended this to be his own tomb he would have occupied the central position. We know that he intended his own tomb to be the tomb of his consort by a bridge; there are indeed traces of the foundations for such a building across the Yamuna River.

This is only a misconception according to some scholars. The idea belongs more to fiction than to history. The Taj Mahal was copleted in 1648 A.D. obviously if any construction had been undertaken on the second Taj it could only be dated after 1648 A.D. & much before 1658 when shah Jehan was finally deposed & imprisoned. The idea seems to be too fanciful & romantic to be historical. Lahuri & Kambo, the contemporary Persian chronicles, do not make the slightest mention of such a plan. The traces which are identified as the foundations of the second Taj can least be associated this way. The masonary structure which extends to the west of the Mehtab Burj is not a foundation but the enclosing wall of the Mehtab Bagh (garden) which was founded by Emperor Babur. Plinth of some pavilions, water channels, tanks, stone slabs, loose brackets & other features are districtly traceable in the adjoining area. As a matter of fact, they mark the site which was occupied & relaid as Charbaghs by Babur & his nobles as his memoirs record.

The irregular position of Shah Jehan's cenotaph in comparision to Mumtaz Mahal's is similar to that at the tomb of Itmad-ud-Daulah, & thus should not be of any striking singnificance. Besides, according to Islamic law, bodies are buried with their faces towards the south, & the husband is placed on the right hand side of his wife. The interpretation that the cenotaph of Shah Jehan was not meant to be placed here appears to be superfluous.

A longstanding popular tradition holds that an identical mausoleum complex was originally supposed to be built on the other side of the river, in black marble instead of white. The story suggests that Shah Jahan was overthrown by his son Aurangzeb before the black version could be built. Ruins of dark marble found across the river are, the story suggests, the unfinished base of this black Taj Mahal.Recent scholarship disputes this theory, and throws some interesting light on the design of the Taj. All other major Mughal tombs were sited in gardens that form a cross, with the tomb at the intersection of the vertical and horizontal pieces. The Taj gardens, by contrast, form a great 'T', with the tomb at the centre of the crosspiece but the outline of the ruins on the other river bank would extend the design of the Taj gardens to form a cross of proportions typical of other Mughal tombs. Further, the marble in the ruins opposite the Taj, while dark from staining, were originally white. In addition, an octagonal pool in these ruins would have reflected the Taj. Scholars have called these ruins the Mahtab bagh or 'Moon light Garden'.

Topic 10:- Legends of Sinking Taj Mahal: - Save the Taj:- It Sinks:-

The site on which the Taj Mahal presently stands marks a point where the Yamuna River takes a sharp curve with the least thrust of water & accurately faces the east. It thus fulfilled all the three requirements & was consequntly selected. Mortar was specially prepared for the purpose with perfectly slaked lime & 'vajra kankar' in equal proportions along with some country ingredients like 'gur, urd-pulse, batashe, besan, rumi-mastagi, belgiri-water', jute and gum. The cementing agent which had thus been prepared was very strong & enduring. The brick was reduced from the standard Mughal size of 8" x7 ½" x1 ¾ "to 7" x 4 ½"x1" so that the 'vajra' mortar could occupy a greater cubic volume of the construction than that which could be filled with the brick. Perfectly baked bricks of first class quality were selected. They were fed into hot fat, mixed with some chemicals, which were absorbed into the porous body of the brick. This thin, almost imperceptible, overcoat made the bricks adequately water proof. Taj Mahal is situated at a point where the dangerous thrust of water would be at a minimum due to sharp curve of river yamuna towards east.

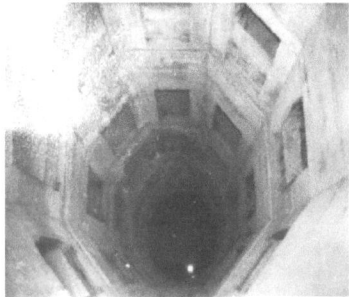

The Interior water well at Taj Mahal

The sepulchre was built at the edge of a stylobate which origenally sloped into the river. Very deep foundations were dug which extended right down to rock level. The system of well foundation was adapted a very scientifically as was the Mughal custom. The plans were prepared with the utmost care, localising the load & the distribution of the weight on the massive piers. The foundations were raised in accordance with the superstructure so that each massive pier could rest on one series of wells which were connected together by means of stong arches. Each well is composed of a massive circular wall of kakai bricks & lime mortar of great strength with axles & spokes placed in it at regular intervals along the whole depth. The core was filled with rubble mixed with mortar. The space between the wells was filled with solid masonry composed of stones & lime.

The load was evenly distributed & passed down to the foundations without the slightest apprehension of cost was taken to provide the huge mass above with a firm & compact base, which origenally rose to a height of 16 shahajahanian yards, equivalent to 43 feets (13.11 metres) from the river Yamuna level. While each massive pier carrying the huge load above it rested directly on a series of wells, the whole was so bonded together as to make it a perfectly compact body. The well foundation had its advantages near the water in as much it minimized the danger from displacement of soil, uneven distribution of the weight & unequal settlement. To counteract the inevitable thrust of water, wells were also piled towards the riverside outside the foundations at close intervals. The wells are in series of three, seven & seventeen & concentrate in large numbers near the north-west corner of the building,i.e.,the Basai Burj where the apprehension of the dangerous thrust of water was the greatest. they have also been distributed, though sparsely, along the whole northen side of the building. This well foundation is a cientific feature of Mughal architecture used almost invariably in all buildings constructed on the river bank, e.g., t Rambagh, Chini-ka Rauza, the tomb of Itmad-ud-Daulah at Agra & others.

'he greatest advantage of this expedient on the external side is that it faces & neutralises the thrust of water efore the latter can do any harm to the building, it counteracts the thrust almost like a living organ as it remains floats intact, even when it is dislodged at its base.Overlaid with mud & sand which the river deposited every year 1ese wells provided an invincible shield to the building. Taj Mahal load uniformly distributed throughout according ɔ principle which is known as the 'cone of incidence' in modern architecture. The load is not allowed to oncentrate at any one point or to rest unevenly.

3ut now the Taj Mahal Monument has been subject to alarming damage, e.g., the cracks, the inclination of the linth & an undeniably dangerous inclination of the minarets, proves that something has gone seriously & xtraordinary wrong with the foundations. Increasing inclination of minarets is alarming. The slop towards the orthen side adds to the apprehension. The cracks have developed to a dangerous magnitude in the second story, 1ainly on the apex of the vaults & ceilings, in the underground chambers & also in & around the base of the 1assive piers near the marble plinth of the main tomb. Here the marble slabs have sometimes been crushed to ieces. All this proves that something has gone seriously wrong with the foundations. It is not due to some leakage f water into the foundations, nor is it due to the shock of some underground movement. In both these cases the racks would have traveled continuously from one storey to another, they would not localize abundantly in the ubterranean vaults & next in the second storey.

: is, it appears, on account of the sinking of the whole massive edifice towards the riverside. A structure which tands at the end of a stylobate just on the edge of water has a natural tendency to move towards the more open ide, the higher edge always acting as a strong buttress, thrusting it in the opposite direction. There is no doubt 1at the builders of the taj were conscious of the whole mass together with the very best materials, into a compact ody.

'hat is what can justifiably be concluded from the available data. It is inconceivable that the builders of the Taj eliberately gave an inclination in the horizontal axis of the marble plinth. Each of the four sides of the marble linth. Each of the four sides of the marble plinth around the mausoleum has its own gargoyles for the discharge of ain-water, thus there is slope respectively on each side & not on the riverside alone. This disproves the theory that 1e architect inclined the plinth deliberately. That the inclination is on the horizontaaxis of the plinth is a sufficient roof that it is inclining towards the river Yamuna as a whole. The inclination of the minarets may be on account of 1e same reason. The displacement of the central axis along its elevation in each case however differs. The nature f this difference has yet to be ascertained. The inclination of the minarets is increasing in each case.

: however began with the displacement of soil beneath the foundations on the riverside. It is the whole mass, and ɪot a part of it that is very gradually sinking. This is what can justifiably be concluded from the available data. So 1er is always questions:-

Vill the architect of the Taj Mahal have to pay such a high price for selecting the site so near the river?

Vill deceitful nature be allowed to play so ruthlessly with the Taj?

Vill this grand majestic memorial be left to its fate to crumble down & vanish into the cruel waters of Yamuna River?

'he Taj Mahal is an important part of our cultural heritage. It is the representation-the reorientation-of well tried ɪrchitectural values which has brought about its incarnation. Posterity will never forgive us if we fail to preserve it & ɔ pass it down to coming generations as it has been passed down to us from last more than 300 years.

Topic 11:- Was The Taj Mahal a Rajput Palace?

History, if we define it in a simplest way, is an impartial study of man's past activities, social, materialistic, asthetic & spiritual, in which we examine all the available sources like, arceological, architectural, epigraphically, numismatic (Coinage), literary, chronicles & accounts of foreign travelers, contemporary & later contemporary, original & secondary, compare one with the other & thus deduce the ultimate truth. It is an objective pursuit as far as practicable. An observation, conclusion or statement, to be a piece of history, should not be based on imagination or conjecture, fiction or fantasy, personal likes & dislikes, taste or interests, but solely on historical data, evaluated with a view to find out the truth which is not anticipated in most cases. This is thus a difficult study, more so in the asthetic & spirtual fields of arts, architecture, religion & philosophy, for example, when interpretations of abstract issues are involved & extremely elusive as they are, the conclusions tend more towards subjectivity. It may result in an unnecessary & useless controversy.

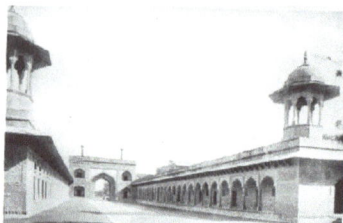

Typical Vedic (Hindu Architecture) style corridors at Taj Mahal

Sources of Hindi literature, too, are silent on the point. It may be noted that Hindi poetry developed exuberantly during the 16th & 17th centuries & produced such savants as Jayasi, Tulsidas & Keshava & scores of other independent litterateurs. The Braj region, in & around Agra, was particularly conducive to progress of the 'Braj Bhasha' poetry & the Ashta-chhap of Vallabhacharya produced some of its greatest poets including, of course, Surdas famous poet. They were devoted to the 'Bhakti' of Lord Krishna wrote independendently. They had no fear or greed. An interesting episode may be mentioned in proof. A poet was forcibly summoned from Vrindaban near Mathura by Emperor Akbar & commanded to recite a verse. What he recited was an apparent insult to the Emperor:

"Santan ko kaha Sikri son kam!

Avat-jat paniyan tutin, Chhot gayo har-nam!

Jake dekhe ghin upjat hai, tahi karve padi Salam!!"

(What we recluses have to do with Fatehpur Sikri, the seat of the Mughal Emperor? We broke our shoes in this journey & had to give up God's name. We had to pay respect to a person whose very sight evokes aversion).

Akbar, however, let him go unpanished. Ti is surprising that no Hindi litterateur noticed a gigantic marble palace at Agra either existing or being built by Man Singh or anyone else & nobody has mentioned it being converted by Shah Jehan into a tomb. The Rajput mansabdars who resided at the capital, the Darul-khilaphat Akbarabad (Agra), had constant communication with their parent states & sent regular messages. These letters are recorded in various Akhabarat (Newspaper) which are preserved. Not a single document mentions, or even makes the slightest allusion, that Raja Man Singh of Ambar(Jaipur) constructed a beautiful palace of white marble on the river-bank at Agra, or that any such structure ever existed before his time. Nor is there any reference whatsoever to the conversion later of a Hindu palace into a tomb during Shah Jehan's region in any of these letters. If a magnificient structure of the Taj Mahal's dimensions had existed or if it had been built by Man Singh & later converted, the fact would have definitely been mentioned in these Rajput records for the writers had no reason to ignore it, or to uppress or conceal this information of such vital importance.

Abdul Hamid Lahauri recorded the events of the first twenty years of the region of shah Jehan in his 'Badshah-Namah'. Muhammad Amin Qazwini, popularly called Aminai Qazwini, wrote the history of the first ten years of Shah Jehan's reign. Her are other independent & equaly trustworthy accounts of Shah Jehan's period among which the 'Shahjahan-Nama' of Inyat Khan. 'Amal-i-Salih' of Kambo, 'Lubbu't tawarikh-i-Hind' of Rai Bhara mal,'Muntakhab-ul-Lubab' of Muhammad Hashim Khafi Khan & the 'Khulasat-ut-Taarkh' of Subhan Rai are the most important. None of these historians makes the slightest mention that shaha Jehan forcibly occupiedany 'imagined' grand palace of Man Singh & converted it into a tomb for his deceased consort Mumtaz Mahal. On the contrary they all give a detailed description of how the Emperor resolved to construct a grand memorial for his beloved Queen & how the building was raised from its very foundations. Particular notice should be taken of the accounts of Lahauri & Kambo. The former mentions that on the 17th of Ziqad (Wednesday) in the year 1040 A.H. (1630 A.D.), Mumtaj Mahal who was with the king at Burhanpur delivered a child & fell ill. She subsequently died & was buried in the Zainabad garden temporarily. Kambo who wrote a complete history of Shah Jehan confirmed that the place in which mumtaz was buried was a piece of land only & was owned by Raja Jaisingh to whom another piece of land given in exchange, later after completion of entire tomb from very begning by well foundations & new construction Mumtaj Mahal finally buried here from temporary Zainabad garden.

All the Persian chronicles confirm that the Taj was constructed on the orders of Shah Jahan & was raised from its very foundations. The fact that the land originally belonged to Raja Man Singh has been recorded but this does not mean that there was a magnificent palace of marble standing on it in 1631 A.D. & which Shaha Jahan converted into a tomb by slight alterations. The assumption is not supported historically & is entirely fictitious. Many European travelers came to Agra between 1580 & 1668. Their accounts help us in reconstructing the history of medieval India, particularly when the Persian chronicler is branded as a biased courtier & is rejected as unreliable. Sir Thomas Roe of England attended the court for more than three years (September 1615 to February 1619) & accompanied Emperor Jehangir wherever he went. De Laet, the Dutch factor, who was at Agra in 1628-29, has left a valuable record of his stay there. He was an accurate & careful observer & his accounts are thoroughly trustworthy. Tavernier, the French jeweler, was in Agra during 1640-41 on his second voyage to the East in India & has described the buildings of Agra at length. But neither has made reference to a white marble palace of Raja Man Singh on the river bank.

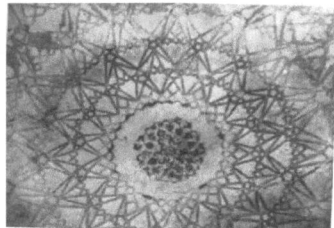

Vedic design on ceiling of a locked room at Taj Mahal

No Culture or civilization & to deny that Emperor Shah Jehan came with a simple monotheistic religion & brought with him the principles of social equality & universal brotherhood, the principles of practical politics- the ability to rule being the only qualification for accession to the throne & the conception of the "Darul-khilafat" or a supreme ruler for the whole world, by adapting same he build the world fame Taj Mahal. The architectural evidence at the Taj Mahal does not show, by any stretch of imagination, that it was originally a Rajput palace. As has already been described, it was fundamentally planned & designed to be a Mughal mausoleum. Their spirit, which brought about a fruition of this art, is writ large on all these Mughal monuments, in the language of stone. Due to only this & majority of his constructed buildings in white marble Emperor Shaha Jahan's period of ruling is known as 'Golden age of architecture' in the history & whole world.

Topic 12:- Was The Taj Mahal a Shiva Temple?

Taj Mahal other Facts as per Prof. P. N. Oak:-

No one has ever challenged it except Prof. P. N. Oak, who believes the whole world has been duped. In his book Taj Mahal: The True Story, Oak says the Taj Mahal is not Queen Mumtaz's tomb but an ancient Hindu temple palace of Lord Shiva (then known as *Tejo Mahalaya*). In the course of his research Oak discovered that the Shiva temple palace was usurped by Shah Jahan from then Maharaja of Jaipur, Jai Singh. In his own court chronicle, Badshahnama, Shah Jahan admits that an exceptionally beautiful grand mansion in Agra was taken from Jai Singh for Mumtaz's burial.

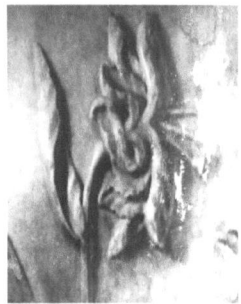

The OM in the flowers on the walls at Taj Mahal

The ex-Maharaja of Jaipur still retains in his secret collection two orders from Shah Jahan for surrendering the Taj building. Using captured temples and mansions, as a burial place for dead courtiers and royalty was a common practice among Muslim rulers. For example, Humayun, Akbar, Etmud-ud-Daula and Safdarjung are all buried in such mansions. Oak's inquiries began with the name of Taj Mahal. He says the term "Mahal "has never been used for a building in any Muslim countries from Afghanistan to Algeria."The unusual explanation that the term Taj Mahal derives from Mumtaz Mahal was illogical in at least two respects. Firstly, her name was never Mumtaz Mahal but **Mumtaz-ul-Zamani**," he writes. Secondly, one cannot omit the first three letters 'Mum' from a woman's name to derive the remainder as the name for the building."Taj Mahal, he claims, is a corrupt version of Tejo Mahalaya, or **Lord Shiva's Palace**. Oak also says the love story of Mumtaz and Shah Jahan is a fairy tale created by court sycophants, blundering historians and sloppy archaeologists Not a single royal chronicle of Shah Jahan's time corroborates the love story.

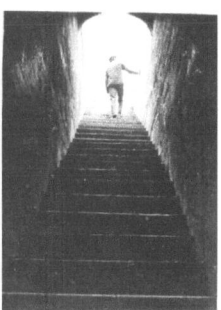

Staircase that leads to the lower levels of Taj Mahal

Furthermore, Oak cites several documents suggesting the Taj Mahal predates Shah Jahan's era, and was a temple dedicated to Shiva, worshipped by Rajputs of Agra city. For example, Prof. Marvin Miller of New York took a few samples from the riverside doorway of the Taj. **Carbon dating tests** revealed that the door was 300 years older than Shah Jahan. European traveler Johan Albert Mandelslo, who visited Agra in 1638 (only seven years after Mumtaz's death), describes the life of the cit y in his memoirs. But he makes no reference to the Taj Mahal being built. The writings of Peter Mundy, an English visitor to Agra within a year of Mumtaz's death, also suggest the Taj was a noteworthy building well before Shah Jahan's time. Prof. Oak points out a number of design and architectural inconsistencies that support the belief of the Taj Mahal being a typical Hindu temple rather than a mausoleum. Many rooms in the Taj Mahal have remained sealed since Shah Jahan's time and are still inaccessible to the public. Oak asserts they contain a headless statue of Lord Shiva and other objects commonly used for worship rituals in Hindu temples fearing political backlash, Indira Gandhi's government tried to have Prof. Oak's book withdrawn from the bookstores, and threatened the Indian publisher of the first edition dire consequences. There is only one way to discredit or validate Oak's research.

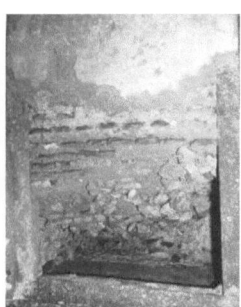

Secret bricked door of Taj Mahal at under ground that hides more evidence

Topic 13:- Myths of Taj Mahal:-

BBC says about Taj Mahal --- Hidden Truth - Never say it is a Tomb

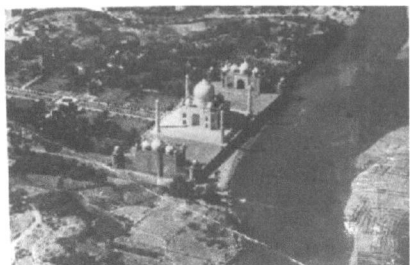

Aerial view of the Taj Mahal

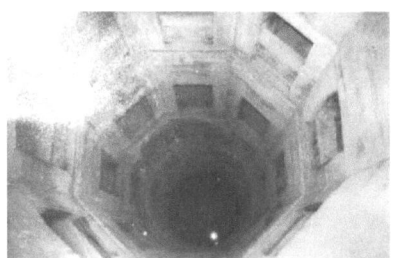

The interior water well

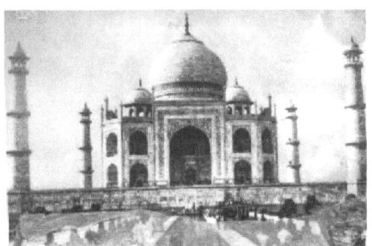

Frontal view of the Taj Mahal and dome

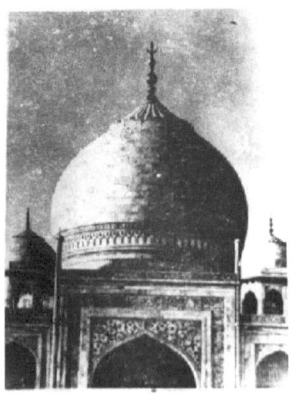

Close up of the dome with pinnacle

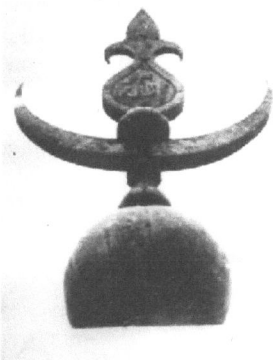

Close up of the pinnacle

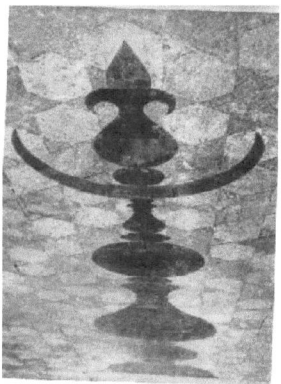

Inlaid pinnacle pattern in courtyard

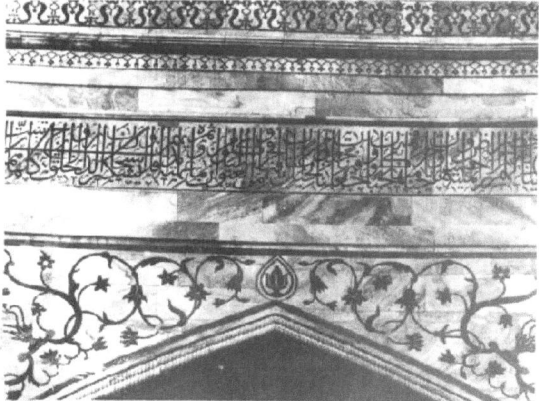

Red lotus at apex of the entrance

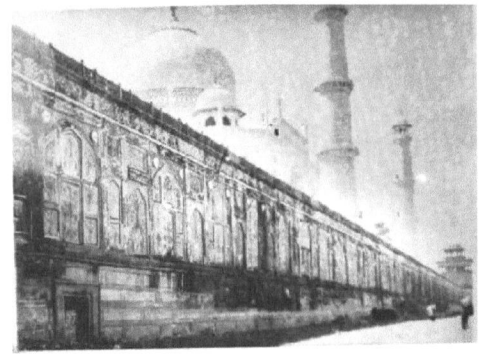

Rear view of the Taj & 22 apartments

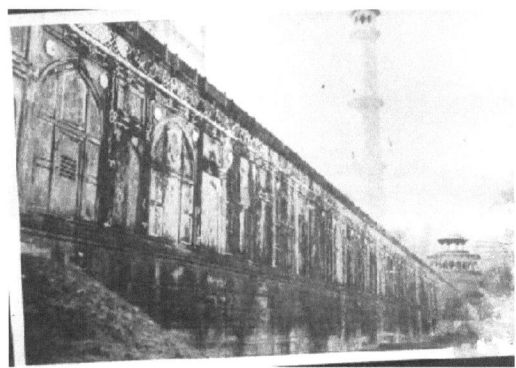

View of sealed doors & windows in back

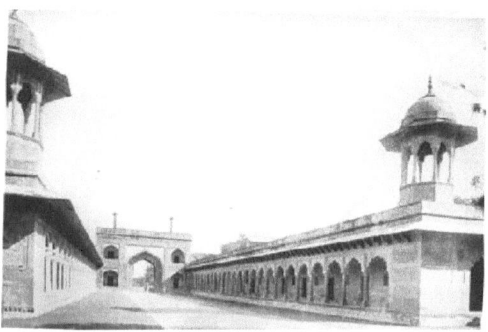

Typical Vedic style corridors

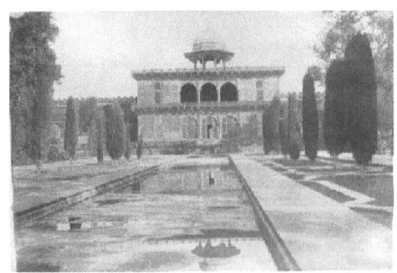

The Music House--a contradiction

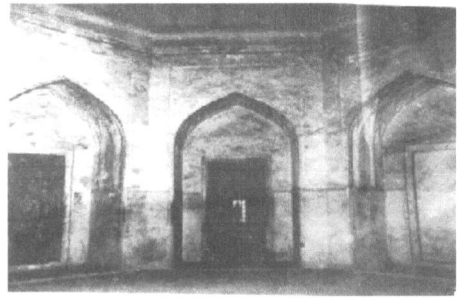

A locked room on upper floor

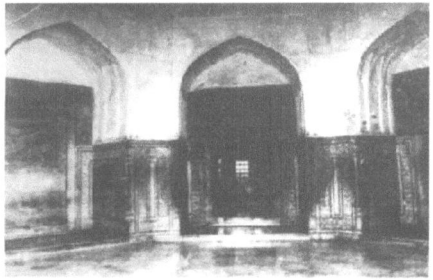

A marble apartment on ground floor

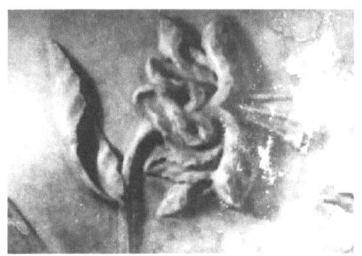

The OM in the flowers on the walls

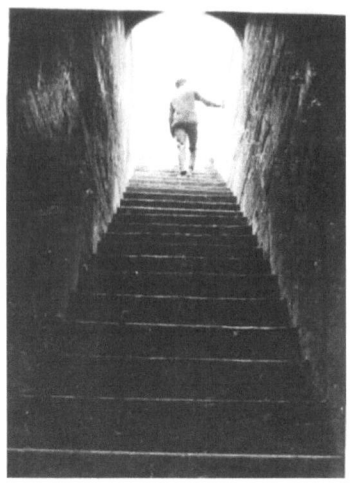

Staircase that leads to the lower levels

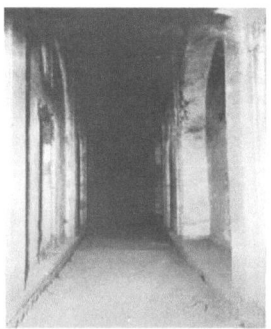

300 foot long corridor inside apartments

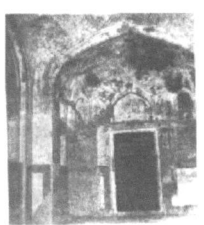

One of the 22 rooms in the secret lower level

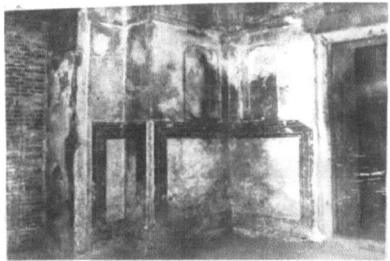

Interior of one of the 22 secret rooms

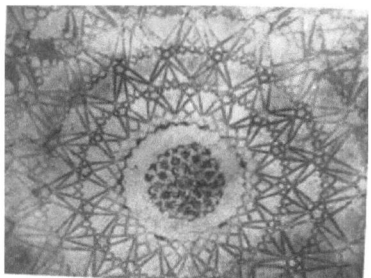

Vedic design on ceiling of a locked room

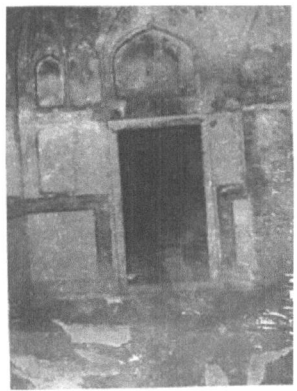

Interior of another of the locked rooms

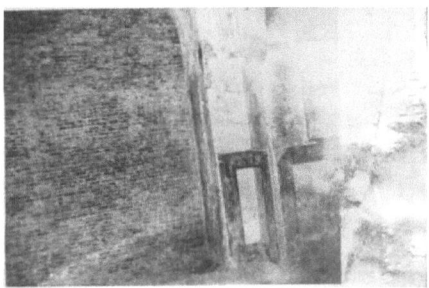

Huge ventilator sealed shut with bricks

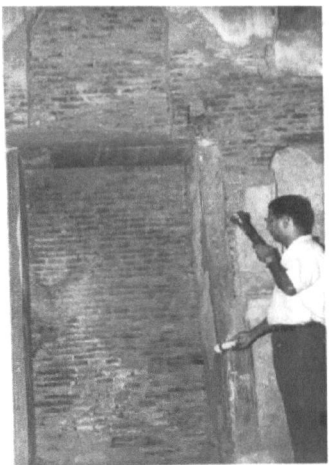

Secret bricked door that hides more evidence

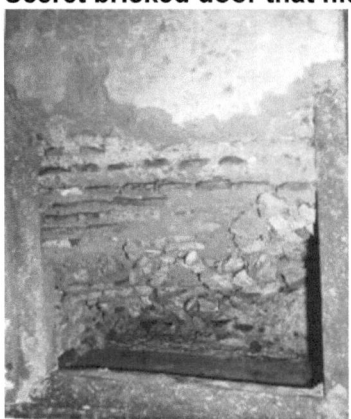

Secret bricked door that hides more evidence

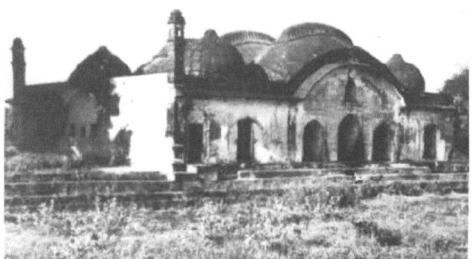

Palace in Barhanpur where Mumtaz died

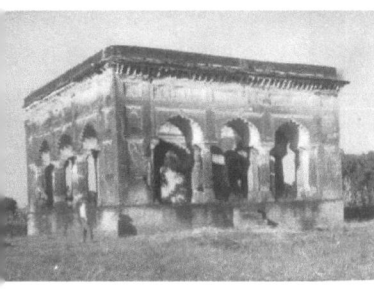

Pavilion where Mumtaz is said to be buried

Taj Mahal other Facts & Myths:-

It is proved Taj Mahal is not a burial of Mumtaj but an ancient temple of Lord Shiva. The Mughal Emperor Shah Jahan in the memory of his wife Mumtaz Mahal built the Taj Mahal. It was built in 22 years (1631 to 1653) by 20,000 artisans brought to India from all over the world! Many people believe Ustad Isa of Iran designed it." This is what your guide probably told you if you ever visited the Taj Mahal. This is the same story I read in my history book as a student.

NOW READ THIS.......

No one has ever challenged it except Prof. P. N. Oak, who believes the whole world has been duped. In his book Taj Mahal: The True Story, Oak says the Taj Mahal is not Queen Mumtaz's tomb but an ancient Hindu temple palace of Lord Shiva (then known as **Tejo Mahalaya**). In the course of his research Oak discovered that the Shiva temple palace was usurped by Shah Jahan from then Maharaja of Jaipur, Jai Singh. In his own court chronicle, Badshahnama, Shah Jahan admits that an exceptionally beautiful grand mansion in Agra was taken from Jai Singh for Mumtaz's burial. The ex-Maharaja of Jaipur still retains in his secret collection two orders from Shah Jahan for surrendering the Taj building. Using captured temples and mansions, as a burial place for dead courtiers and royalty was a common practice among Muslim rulers. For example, Humayun, Akbar, Etmud-ud-Daula and Safdarjung are all buried in such mansions. Oak's inquiries began with the name of Taj Mahal. He says the term Mahal "has never been used for a building in any Muslim countries from Afghanistan to Algeria. "The unusual explanation that the term Taj Mahal derives from Mumtaz Mahal was illogical in at least two respects.

Firstly, her name was never Mumtaz Mahal but Mumtaz-ul-Zamani," he writes. Secondly, one cannot omit the first three letters 'Mum' from a woman's name to derive the remainder as the name for the building".Taj Mahal, he claims, is a corrupt version of Tejo Mahalaya, or Lord Shiva's Palace. Oak also says the love story of Mumtaz and Shah Jahan is a fairy tale created by court sycophants, blundering historians and sloppy archaeologists not a single royal chronicle of Shah Jahan's time corroborates the love story. Furthermore, Oak cites several documents suggesting the Taj Mahal predates Shah Jahan's era, and was a temple dedicated to Shiva, worshipped by Rajputs of Agra city. For example, Prof. Marvin Miller of New York took a few samples from the riverside doorway of the Taj. Carbon dating tests revealed that the door was 300 years older than Shah Jahan. European traveler Johan Albert Mandelslo, who visited Agra in 1638 (only seven years after Mumtaz's death), describes the life of the city in his memoirs. But he makes no reference to the Taj Mahal being built. The writings of Peter Mundy, an English visitor to Agra within a year of Mumtaz's death, also suggest the Taj was a noteworthy building well before Shah Jahan's time. Prof. Oak points out a number of design and architectural inconsistencies that support the belief of the Taj Mahal being a typical Hindu temple rather than a mausoleum. Many rooms in the Taj Mahal have remained sealed since Shah Jahan's time and are still inaccessible to the public. Oak asserts they contain a headless statue of Lord Shiva and other objects commonly used for worship rituals in Hindu temples fearing political backlash, Indira Gandhi's government tried to have Prof. Oak's book withdrawn from the bookstores, and threatened the Indian publisher of the first edition dire consequences. There is only one way to discredit or validate Oak's research.

The current government should open the sealed rooms of the Taj Mahal under U.N. supervision, and let international experts investigate.
Do circulate this to all you know and let them know about this reality..... Please check this link ....it adds as a visual proof.........http://www.stephen-knapp.com/was_the_taj_mahal_a_vedic_temple.htm

There is one Myth about that Emperor Shah Jahan cut workers hands just after the contraction of Taj Mahal, but it is not true. He only suggested to his workers even requested after giving them huge amount of Gold & Silver as their reward for not to built same Taj Mahal like any structure or look alike or same building any where due to making Taj Mahal for its Uniqueness in the World.

Topic 14:- Myth about the sinking Taj Mahal:-

Save the Taj: It Sinks:

The site on which the Taj Mahal presently stands marks a point where the Yamuna River takes a sharp curve with the least thrust of water & accurately faces the east. It thus fulfilled all the three requirements & was consequently selected. Mortar was specially prepared for the purpose with perfectly slaked lime & 'vajra kankar' in equal proportions along with some country ingredients like *'gur, urd-pulse, batashe, besan, rumi-mastagi, belgiri-water'*, jute and gum. The cementing agent which had thus been prepared was very strong & enduring. The brick was reduced from the standard Mughal size of 8" x7 ½" x1 ¾ "to 7" x 4 ½"x1" so that the 'vajra' mortar could occupy a greater cubic volume of the construction than that which could be filled with the brick. Perfectly baked bricks of first class quality were selected. They were fed into hot fat, mixed with some chemicals, which were absorbed into the porous body of the brick. This thin, almost imperceptible, overcoat made the bricks adequately water proof. Taj Mahal is situated at a point where the dangerous thrust of water would be at a minimum due to sharp curve of river yamuna towards east.

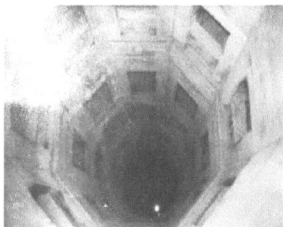

The Interior water well at Taj Mahal

The sepulcher was built at the edge of a stylobate which originally sloped into the river. Very deep foundations were dug which extended right down to rock level. The system of well foundation was adapted a very scientifically as was the Mughal custom. The plans were prepared with the utmost care, localizing the load & the distribution of the weight on the massive piers. The foundations were raised in accordance with the superstructure so that each massive pier could rest on one series of wells which were connected together by means of strong arches. Each well is composed of a massive circular wall of *kakaiya* bricks & lime mortar of great strength with axles & spokes placed in it at regular intervals along the whole depth. The core was filled with rubble mixed with mortar. The space between the wells was filled with solid masonry composed of stones & lime.

The load was evenly distributed & passed down to the foundations without the slightest apprehension of cost was taken to provide the huge mass above with a firm & compact base, which originally rose to a height of 16 shahajahanian yards, equivalent to 43 feets (13.11 metres) from the river Yamuna level. While each massive pier carrying the huge load above it rested directly on a series of wells, the whole was so bonded together as to make it a perfectly compact body. The well foundation had its advantages near the water in as much it minimized the danger from displacement of soil, uneven distribution of the weight & unequal settlement. To counteract the inevitable thrust of water, wells were also piled towards the riverside outside the foundations at close intervals. The wells are in series of three, seven & seventeen & concentrate in large numbers near the north-west corner of the building, i.e., the Basai Burj where the apprehension of the dangerous thrust of water was the greatest. They have also been distributed, though sparsely, along the whole northern side of the building. This well foundation is a scientific feature of Mughal architecture used almost invariably in all buildings constructed on the river bank, e.g., at Rambagh, Chini-ka Rauza, the tomb of Itmad-ud-Daulah at Agra & others.

The greatest advantage of this expedient on the external side is that it faces & neutralizes the thrust of water before the latter can do any harm to the building; it counteracts the thrust almost like a living organ as it remains afloat intact, even when it is dislodged at its base. Overlaid with mud & sand which the river deposited every year these wells provided an invincible shield to the building. Taj Mahal load uniformly distributed throughout according to principle which is known as the 'cone of incidence' in modern architecture. The load is not allowed to concentrate at any one point or to rest unevenly.

But now the Taj Mahal Monument has been subject to alarming damage, e.g., the cracks, the inclination of the plinth & an undeniably dangerous inclination of the minarets, proves that something has gone seriously & extraordinary wrong with the foundations. Increasing inclination of minarets is alarming. The slop towards the northern side adds to the apprehension. The cracks have developed to a dangerous magnitude in the second story, mainly on the apex of the vaults & ceilings, in the underground chambers & also in & around the base of the massive piers near the marble plinth of the main tomb. Here the marble slabs have sometimes been crushed to pieces. All this proves that something has gone seriously wrong with the foundations. It is not due to some leakage of water into the foundations, nor is it due to the shock of some underground movement. In both these cases the cracks would have traveled continuously from one storey to another, they would not localize abundantly in the subterranean vaults & next in the second storey.

It is, it appears, on account of the sinking of the whole massive edifice towards the riverside. A structure which stands at the end of a stylobate just on the edge of water has a natural tendency to move towards the more open side, the higher edge always acting as a strong buttress, thrusting it in the opposite direction. There is no doubt that the builders of the taj were conscious of the whole mass together with the very best materials, into a compact body.

That is what can justifiably be concluded from the available data. It is inconceivable that the builders of the Taj deliberately gave an inclination in the horizontal axis of the marble plinth. Each of the four sides of the marble plinth. Each of the four sides of the marble plinth around the mausoleum has its own gargoyles for the discharge of rain-water, thus there is slope respectively on each side & not on the riverside alone. This disproves the theory that the architect inclined the plinth deliberately. That the inclination is on the horizontaaxis of the plinth is a sufficient proof that it is inclining towards the river Yamuna as a whole. The inclination of the minarets may be on account of the same reason. The displacement of the central axis along its elevation in each case however differs. The nature of this difference has yet to be ascertained. The inclination of the minarets is increasing in each case.

It however began with the displacement of soil beneath the foundations on the riverside. It is the whole mass, and not a part of it that is very gradually sinking. This is what can justifiably be concluded from the available data. So ther is always questions:-

Will the architect of the Taj Mahal have to pay such a high price for selecting the site so near the river?

Will deceitful nature be allowed to play so ruthlessly with the Taj?

Will this grand majestic memorial be left to its fate to crumble down & vanish into the cruel waters of Yamuna River?

The Taj Mahal is an important part of our cultural heritage. It is the representation-the reorientation-of well tried architectural values which has brought about its incarnation. Posterity will never forgive us if we fail to preserve it & to pass it down to coming generations as it has been passed down to us from last more than 300 years.

Topic 15:- Myth about the Black Taj Mahal:-

Story & Legend of Black Taj Mahal of Shah Jahan:

Emperor Shah Jahan according to a popular legend decided to construct another Taj Mahal in black marble on the other side of the Yamuna River & to connect the two by a gold bridge. This structure was intended to be his own tomb. It has been recorded almost contemporarily by a French merchant Tavernier: "Shaha Jehan began to build his own tomb on the other side of the river but the war with his sons interrupted his plan and Auragzeb who reign at present is not disposed to complete it." Later gazetteers & guide books mention 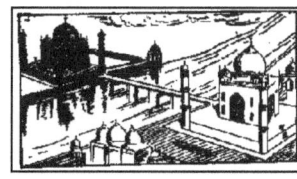 this story almost invariably. The irregular position of the cenotaph of Shah Jehan as compared to that of Mumtaj Mahal which occupies the center of the hall is said to be proof of this assumption. Particularly Moinuddin attached the greatest credence to the legend & went to the extent of pointing out traces of the unmatured plan on the other side. The Mehtab Burj & the walls which adjoin it opposite the Taj Mahal are generally said to be the foundations & remains of the proposed plan. This has been accepted even in the most recent times. J.B. page spoke of it affirmatively. 'Had the Emperor at first intended this to be his own tomb he would have occupied the central position. We know that he intended his own tomb to be the tomb of his consort by a bridge; there are indeed traces of the foundations for such a building across the Yamuna River.

This is only a misconception according to some scholars. The idea belongs more to fiction than to history. The Taj Mahal was completed in 1648 A.D. obviously if any construction had been undertaken on the second Taj it could only be dated after 1648 A.D. & much before 1658 when shah Jehan was finally deposed & imprisoned. The idea seems to be too fanciful & romantic to be historical. Lahuri & Kambo, the contemporary Persian chronicles, do not make the slightest mention of such a plan. The traces which are identified as the foundations of the second Taj can least be associated this way. The masonry structure which extends to the west of the Mehtab Burj is not a foundation but the enclosing wall of the Mehtab Bagh (garden) which was founded by Emperor Babur. Plinth of some pavilions, water channels, tanks, stone slabs, loose brackets & other features are distinctly traceable in the adjoining area. As a matter of fact, they mark the site which was occupied & re-laid as charbaghs by Babur & his nobles as his memoirs record.

The irregular position of Shah Jehan's cenotaph in comparison to Mumtaz Mahal's is similar to that at the tomb of Itmad-ud-Daulah, & thus should not be of any striking significance. Besides, according to Islamic law, bodies are buried with their faces towards the south, & the husband is placed on the right hand side of his wife. The interpretation that the cenotaph of Shah Jehan was not meant to be placed here appears to be superfluous.

A longstanding popular tradition holds that an identical mausoleum complex was originally supposed to be built on the other side of the river, in black marble instead of white. The story suggests that Shah Jahan was overthrown by his son Aurangzeb before the black version could be built. Ruins of dark marble found across the river are, the story suggests, the unfinished base of this black Taj Mahal.Recent scholarship disputes this theory, and throws some interesting light on the design of the Taj. All other major Mughal tombs were sited in gardens that form a cross, with the tomb at the intersection of the vertical and horizontal pieces. The Taj gardens, by contrast, form a great 'T', with the tomb at the centre of the crosspiece but the outline of the ruins on the other river bank would extend the design of the Taj gardens to form a cross of proportions typical of other Mughal tombs. Further, the marble in the ruins opposite the Taj, while dark from staining, were originally white. In addition, an octagonal pool in these ruins would have reflected the Taj. Scholars have called these ruins the Mahtab bagh or 'Moon light Garden'.

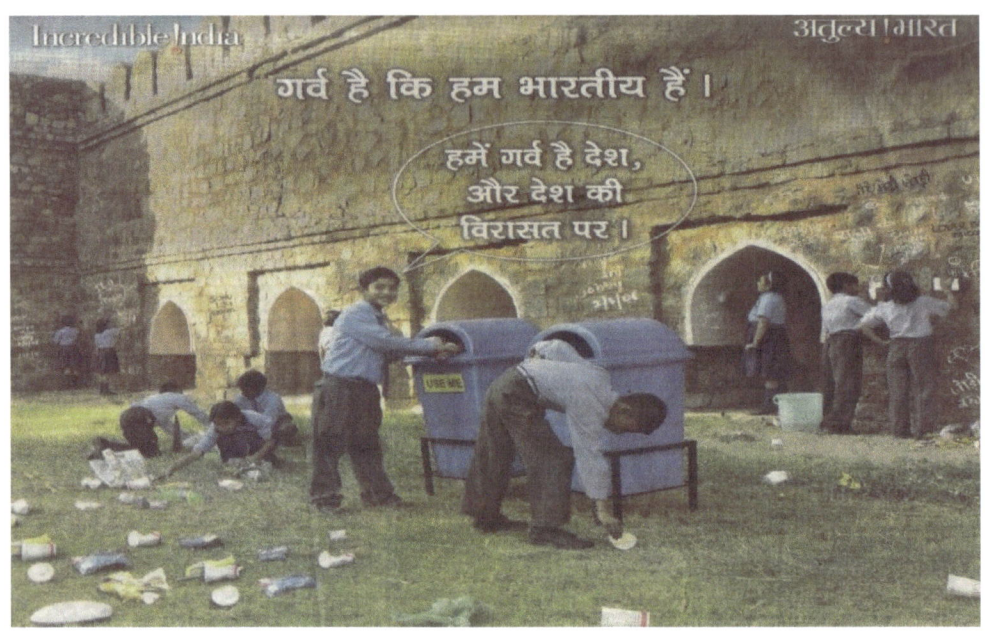

Help to Protect our Priceless Historical Treasure of Heritage Monuments for New coming Generations - By not Destroying, Spitting, putting Garbage and not writing anything on Monuments.

Bibliography: -

(References): -

Writer of Book -Text & Photographs Source: Anurag Mathur, M.A. - History, P. G. Dip. Hotel & Tourism Management, Ph.D. Researcher of History, Travel & Tourism, Advance Course on Tourism from WTO - World Tourism Organization, IITTM -Indian Institute of Tourism & Travel Management, Ministry of Tourism, Govt. of India, New Delhi & Numismatist, Philatelist & Antiques Collector, Lucknow).

Main Source: Father of Author Anurag Mathur, Late. Shri. O.N. Mathur, Archeological Survey of India (ASI), Govt. of India -Posted at Taj Mahal & other Historical Monuments at Agra-1975 - 89. Author Anurag Mathur's forefather was posted at Royal Imperial Court of Emperor Shaha jahan as Finance Minister (Treasury Incharge –*Shahi Khazana*) as per Author's Family Tree Records & generations Chronology & best all ancestors were educated from Kayastha family and served in Royal Mughal Court after one by one.   - - Indian Culture & Heritage Information, Lucknow.

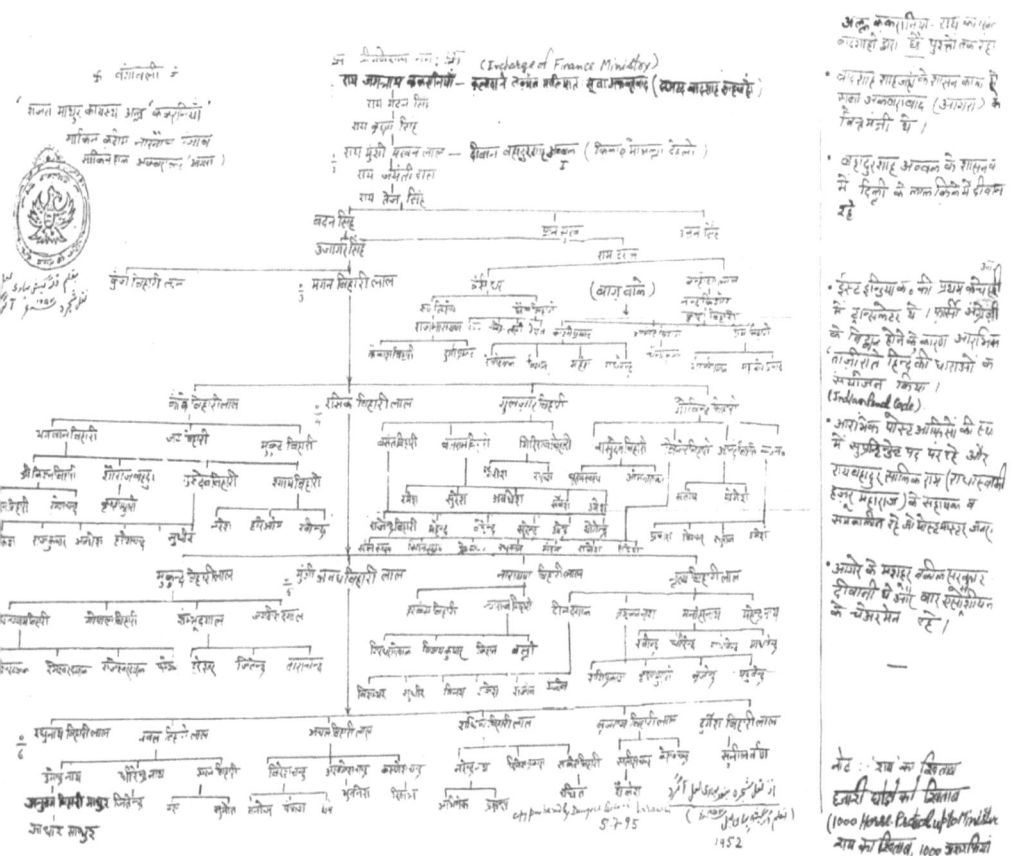

**Family tree of Author Anurag Mathur from Mughal Emperor Shaha Jahan's period (1628 A.D. Onwards) -
Sajra - (In Hindi Language).**

Books & Journals: -
(For More Information)

Archarya, Ram (Ph.D)   -'Tourism and Cultural Heritage of India' Department of Tourism & Hotel Management University of Rajasthan, Jaipur (1980).

Jawaharlal Nehru   -'The Discovery of India' Jawaharlal Nehru Memorial Fund, Oxford University Press, Teen Murti House, New Delhi (1988).

K.C.Mazumdar, H.C.Roy Choudhary-   'An Advanced History of India' Published by Macmillan India Ltd. & K.C.Datta Text based on an advanced History of India, Cyber Multimedia New Delhi

Ram Sharan Sharma   -'Ancient India' National Council of Educational Research and Training. A text book for class XI. New Delhi (1988).

Satish Chandra   -'Medieval India' Part-I & II, National Council of Educational Research and Training. A text book for class XI-XII. New Delhi (1986).

Bipin Chandra   -'Modern India' National Council of Educational Research and Training. A text book for class XI-XII. New Delhi (1971).

Prof. B.C. Rai &   -'Constitutional History of India & National Movement' Prakashan
Prof. L.N. Mukherjee   Kendra, Railway Crossing, Sitapur Road, Lucknow (1987).
Ziyud-din A. Desai   -'Indo-Islamic Architecture' Ministry of Information and
(Director Archeological   Broadcasting, Government of India. New Delhi (1986).
Survey of India, Nagpur)

Dr.Z.A.Desai & H.K.Kaul   -'Taj Museum' Published by the Archeological Survey of India New Delhi (1982).

Mathuram Bhoothalingam   -'Temples of India-Myths and Legends' Ministry of Information And Broadcasting, Government of India.New Delhi (1986).

P.S Joshi & S.V. Gholkar   -'History of the Modern World' (1900-1960), New Delhi (1983).

R. Nath   -Ph.D., D.D.Litt. Lecturer of History Agra College Agra & Fellow

	Of the Indian Council of Historical Research-The Immortal Taj Mahal, 1972, Taraporaevala, Bombay
R.Nath	-'Agra and its Monumental Glory' Taraporevala, Bombay (1977).
J.P.Sinha	-'History of India' (1707 A.D. To Present Day), Q & A, Meerut (1976-77).
Dr.B.R. Kishore	-'Dances of India' Diamond Publications, New Delhi (1988).
B.K.Chaturvedi	-'Dresses & Costumes of India' Diamond Publications, New Delhi (1988).
B.K.Chaturvedi	-'Jewelry of India' Diamond Publications, New Delhi (1988).
	-'Fast and Festivals of India' Diamond Publications, New Delhi (1991).

Multi-Media CD-ROM's: -

K.C.Mazumdar, H.C.Roychoudhary- & K.C.Datta	'An Advanced History of India' Published by Macmillan India Ltd. Text based on an advanced History of India, Cyber Multimedia New Delhi. Email:cybermm@cmil.com Web: http://www.cybermm.com

Websites for more information: -

www.ccrtindia.org	-Complete CCRT site on Indian History & Culture of India, Under Ministry of Culture, Government of India.
www.indiaheritage.com	-Developed & Maintained by Macrographics.com
www.infoplease.com	-World History Site.
www.hindugallery.com	
www.indiansaga.com	-Complete site on Indian History & Culture of India
www.harijanaonline/sanskrit.com	-For Veda's details

www.hindunet.org   -Hindusim best site
www.wikipedia.org   -Complete site on Indian History & Culture of India
www.Mughalgardens.org   -Site of Mughal History
www.vegetarianrestaurens.net   -God & goddess of India site
www.khazana.com
www.visitindia.com
www.raga.com   -Site of Classical Music of India
www.dhrupad.org   -Site of Classical Music of India
www.indianindustry.com   -Handicrafts of Indian Manufactures
www.fordham.edu   -Free Internet History source book
www.aptourism.com   -Andhra Pradesh Tourism site
www.thebritishmuseum.ac.uk   -The British Museum site
www.tradewingtravel.com
www.indialife.com/history/freedomstruggle.htm   -Unique History site
www.culturopidia.com   -Complete site on Indian History & Culture of India

www.india.gov.in   -Complete site on Indian History & Culture of India,
                                         Government of India

www.webdunia.com   -Hindi site of Indian Culture, God & Goddess of India
www.indiataste.com

www.san.beck.org   -Hindu Philosophy.

www.cdac.in/html/ihportal/index.asp#1http   -Indian Heritage Portal.

www.indtravel.com   -Site for Photo Albam of India & Cultural Heritage.

www.eholidaysindia.com/images/pilgrimagetop.jpg

                                         -Site for Photo Albam of India & Cultural Heritage.

www.tanjoreart.com   -Site for Paintings of India & Cultural Heritage.

www.indiaplaza.com   -Site for Paintings of India & Cultural Heritage.

www.craftsindia.com   -Site for Paintings-Handicrafts of India & Cultural Heritage.

giniann.wordpress.com   -Site for Indian Cuisines

www.indiasite.com   -Site for Indian Cuisines

surfinamma.com   -Site for Medals & Badges

http://stamps.listings.ebay.in/Coins-Notes_Indian-Coins

-Site for Coins, Medals & Badges

Related Links for more information: -

www.festivalsofindia.com   -Best all Festivals of Inida site.

www.indiaculture.nic.in

www.asi.nic.in   -Archeological survey of India, Govt.of India.

www.ignca.nic.in   -Indra Gandhi National centre for Arts & Culture.

www.lalitkaka.gov.in   -Lalit Kala Academy

www.nationalachives.nic.in   -National Archives.

www.nlindia.org   -National Library, Deptt. of Culture

www.razalibrary.com   -Raza Library, Rampur.

www.nationalmuseumindia.org -National Museum, New Delhi.

www.nationmaster.com   -History & Economic History site.

www.indiatravelogue.com   -Travel & Tourism site.

www.yoursmenindia.com

www.ttkbharatplanet.com

www.san.beck.org   -Hindu philosophy site.

www.historychannel.com   -TV History Channel Site.

www.indiaplaza.com

www.indiatourism.com

www.incredibleindia.org   -Government of India Culture site.

www.atributetohindusim.com

www.kamatpotpuri.com

www.culturalindia.com

www.arangham.com   -Dance site

www.indiasite.com   -Site for Geography details of India & Tours.

www.sanjivkapoor.com   -Site for Cuisines of India with Recipes.

www.chefs.com   -Recipe Site.

www.starware.com   -Recipe Site.

www.indianmirror.com

www.ua.nic.in/uttaranchaltourism -Uttaranchal Tourism site.

www.dihrm.com   -Site for Delhi Institute of **Heritage Research & Management.**

www.india.gov.in
History of Sultanate Architecture, 1967, Delhi
www.infoplease.com/ world history
indiatravelogue.com
http://www.sscnet.ucla.edu/southasia/History.

Disclaimer

This disclaimer is made on behalf of me, its affiliates and its third party information and service providers ("Service Providers") together with any of these entities officers, employees, directors, or agents. All information contained herein is obtained by me from sources believed by in travel to be accurate and reliable and every effort is taken to verify, correct and update the information provided in this site at the time of uploading. Because of the possibility of human and mechanical error as well as other factors or omissions, we cannot accept responsibility for any authenticity of the data provided, travel information, rules and conditions that are incorrectly represented within this system. I or the Service Providers' make any warranty regarding the correctness or reliability of the information and all information is provided "as is".

The authenticity of the data provided is to be verified by one who is planning to use the information, as they are bound to change. I and its Service Providers make no representations and subject to below, disclaim all express, implied, and statutory warranties of any kind to user and/or any third party including warranties as to accuracy, timeliness, completeness, merchantability, or fitness for any particular purpose.

My self and its Service Providers shall under no circumstance be liable to you, and/or any third party for any lost profits or lost opportunity, indirect, special, consequential, incidental, or punitive damages whatsoever, even it has been advised of the possibility of such damages.

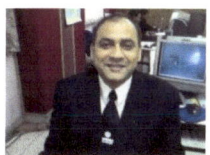

About Author: - Anurag Mathur (B.Sc., M.A. - History, PhD Level Research, Post Graduate Diploma in Hotel & Tourism Management Advance Course in Tourism from IITTM – Indian Institute of Tourism & Travel Management- Ministry of Tourism Govt. of India, New Delhi & WTO (World Tourism Organization). PGDBIM MBA-Delhi). Ex. Lecturer of History, Hotel & Tourism Management Department at Agra University. Agra & also Numismatist (Coins Collector), Philatelist, Antiques, Rare Photographs & Paintings Collector etc, Lucknow. U.P. India.

Father of Author Anurag Mathur, Late. Shri. O.N. Mathur, Archeological Survey of India (ASI), Govt. of India -Posted at Taj Mahal & other Historical Monuments at Agra-1975 - 89. Author Anurag Mathur's forefather was posted at Royal Imperial Court of Emperor Shaha jahan as Finance Minister (Treasury Incharge –*Shahi Khazana*) as per Author's Family Tree Records & generations Chronology & rest all ancestors were educated from Kayastha family and served in Royal Mughal Court after one by one.   - - Indian Culture & Heritage Information, Lucknow.

ISBN-13: 9781540552402
ISBN -10: 1540552403

would greatly appreciate any contribution - even a very small one.

Please write to Anurag Mathur

ANURAG MATHUR

Indian Culture & Heritage Information
Business, Research & Development
Lucknow. U.P. PIN-226024. INDIA

E-mail: anurag5551@hotmail.com, anuragmathu@gmail.com.

www.ingramcontent.com/pod-product-compliance
Lightning Source LLC
Chambersburg PA
CBHW040832180526
45159CB00001B/159